All Lines In

Find More Buyers, Sell More Homes

The Marketing Strategy Playbook for Residential New Home Builders and Developers

Robert Cowes III

SmartTouch® Interactive
President & CEO

Editing by Rebecca Eddleman.
Cover design by Shawn Ng.
Illustration & Image Credits: P. 118

ISBN: 9781689129053

SmartTouch® Interactive
8500 Shoal Creek Blvd
Bldg. 4, Ste 100
Austin, TX 78757

(512) 582-5900
rcowes@smarttouchinteractive.com
www.smarttouchinteractive.com

What they say about Robert...

"Robert and his team at SmartTouch® have been instrumental in expanding our company from 10 home closings to over 200 in just 4 years working together. Our decision to buy into Robert's digital marketing and sales pipeline management strategies has been the most important factor driving our growth."

- **Nick Rhodes – President, Esperanza Homes**

"In my search to find a complete solution to digital marketing for my production home building business, there was only one company that combines Contact Resource Management (CRM), digital content creation, and media advertisement placement. Not only does SmartTouch® create order out of a digital world of chaos, they bring accountability to marketing budgets and analytics to show where the buyers are coming from. They have been an integral part of Saratoga Homes Houston's business now for over 6 years. Robert Cowes and Tanner Ross of SmartTouch® have a secret sauce of digital advertising that is hard to find. Keep it up!"

- **Jack Bombach – COO, Saratoga Homes**

"Robert is incredibly talented at finding unique and innovative ways to market homes. Robert and his team have seen it all and will help you sell more homes in the most competitive market."

- **David Blackburn - CEO, The Blackburn Group, LLC**

"I have found Robert to be a phenomenal resource of knowledge in a very dynamic industry. His state-of-the-art approach and unique informational gathering techniques have been instrumental to our growth as a company."

- **Chris Wales - Division President, Blackburn Communities**

"Robert Cowes is at the forefront of the real estate industry and digital marketing. Over the last 4 years, Robert and I have worked together on a number of projects and he has helped me generate thousands of leads that have resulted in sales and millions of dollars for my companies. Robert Cowes can help build your business if you are open to new ideas and allow him to show you the way. Robert's strategies are the future of real estate."

- **Erika Ramon - Director of Marketing, Randolph Todd Development**

Table of Contents

Acknowledgements

Thank you to the following **mentors and executives** for the opportunity to be your marketing partner and allowing SmartTouch® Interactive to become great guides in your home building business and helping to improve your sales and marketing efficiency.

Thank you, Jeff Novak, CEO, Novak Brothers (Mentorship)
Thank you, Jack Bombach COO, Saratoga Homes (Client – Role Model)
Thank you, Nick Rhodes President, Esperanza Homes (Client – Role Model)
Thank you, David Blackburn, CEO, Blackburn Communities (Client – Role Model)

Thank you and fabulous job to our **editor-in-chief** who helped bring this book to publication.

Rebecca Eddleman
beccamary.content@gmail.com

To God
To el Nazareno de Portobelo
To My Family Los Cowes
To the SmartTouch® Team
To Friends & Peers
To Austin & Panama, My Two Homes
& To All the Dedicated Fisherman Marketers

Many blessings, always.

40+ Real Estate Creative Marketing Awards HBA, NAHB, TBA

A Fishing Story

Most new home builders realize that their success in launching and selling the homes in their developments will require some marketing effort. They can expect the need to go "fishing" for new home buyers. Well, there's a lot we can learn about "fishing" for new home buyers from three builders who did just that. Three builders get into a boat...

Three builders, who develop their own land/communities planned a get together for a guys' fishing trip and retreat. They decided to make it interesting and waged a bottle of their favorite spirit. Since Easter was approaching, they decided victory would go to the one that caught enough fish to feed their family during the entire Lenten season.

Fisherman 1 and 2 go fishing on occasion once or twice a year, and they both grew up fishing, so they brought their favorite tried-and-true tackle and favorite rods. Fisherman 3 was not really experienced and decided to do some research on the lake, the fish that inhabit it, and the area conditions. In doing so, he realized that there were many moving parts, and he didn't want to take the risk of losing. So, utilizing the same decision-making criteria that he used in making land deals, he waged his bet by getting the area's best fishing guide to assure he fulfilled his mission – getting enough fish to last the Lenten season.

They arrived at the lake cabin and Fisherman 1 and 2 poked fun at how Fisherman 3 had no fishing skills compared to their experience and proclaimed expertise. But what he did have with him, was a fishing guide. Fisherman 1 and 2 laughed at Fisherman 3 for needing a guide and teased him for not learning the ropes on his own. Fisherman 3 remained unphased by their teasing and declared to his fishing buddies that he wasn't going to risk losing because he was afraid to splurge on the expert help that would give him a competitive edge. Fisherman 1 and 2 laughed, thinking that only "losers" needed to pay for extra help to get the job done. But Fisherman 3 knew that this fishing challenge was a lot like being stuck with an unsold inventory of homes. Losing to these guys would be like having 200-day old unsold inventory. That's when he decided to invest in the expert help—as he imagined feasting over enough fish to last until Easter.

The next day, the wager commenced. Fisherman 1 and 2 got some early morning bites and a couple of small ones, but no keepers. In the middle of the day they had some equipment failure with their rusty "tried-and-true" tackle and ended up losing valuable day time. Fisherman 3 entered the water a little later in the day, met his guide, and off they went to the lake's best "honey holes."

By 11:00 am, Fisherman 3 was done for the day, having caught his limit, he called it a day. When they all got back to the cabin for lunch, Fisherman 3 realized his two buddies had gotten skunked compared to what he was able to catch in a limited few hours. He knew that by fishing smarter and investing in the right expertise, he wasn't going to go home empty handed. By the end of the weekend, it was clear that Fisherman 3 had clearly caught more than enough fish to last the Lenten season. Victory was his. He knew that with the help of his expert guide, all his lines were positioned in the best spots, with the best tools.

As the three fishermen lifted their glasses to toast the victor, Fisherman 3 teased, "There's no sense in fishing unless you plan on catching something! And if you want to catch more than something, it pays to invest in an expert guide who knows the area's particular waters and fish in order to have a competitive edge."

Are You in the New "Home Building" or New "Home Selling" Business?

When you go out to a social event and meet a new person, and they ask, "What do you do for a living?" your typical answer is going to be, "I'm in the home building business." But, are you really? You probably buy your home designs from an architect, subcontract the build-out to trades, and ultimately, take on the task of selling the homes for as much as you can, as fast as you can. This is what really makes the business work. So, I pose the question again, are you really in the *"home building"* business? WRONG! You're in the *"home selling"* business.

The residential home builder and developer's true business play is to build a sales and marketing machine that can generate product absorption and a sales velocity that aligns with the ROI goals of their business deals. If you believe this principal, then you know there are 5 key variables for success in the home selling business: the land deal, the product, the price point, demand/economic factors, and marketing.

Believing in these principles, you spend countless hours studying the site and market conditions, dealing with city governments, understanding demographics, spending tens of thousands of dollars on designing the right product; all in an effort to align risk and reward to convince management, investors, bankers, and equity holders that the risk is worth the reward. Yet, the 5th variable, the "M" word, is often confined to work with ONLY 1% or less of gross revenue and expected to deliver results that are better than the competition. In other words, 1 of the 5 critical components to a deal's success is assigned a microscopic budget of just 1% of gross revenue.

Why? Is it because that's the way it's always been in your firm and it's worked? Does 90% of your business come from realtors? If that is acceptable to you, you need to face the reality that you are entering the fiercest battle in the history of the "home selling business." In this digital marketing era, buyers have immediate access to all of the relevant data needed to make home buying decisions at their fingertips—on their smartphone, iPad/tablet, or desktop—or with a single command to "Alexa."

You are competing in an age in which every builder, developer, and agent has a website, targeted landing pages, and dedicated mobile websites for the growing mobile audience. Publishers of real estate listings such as Trulia, Zillow, New Home Source, Builders Update, New Homes Directory, Homes.com, Hot on Homes, RedFin, and every MLS system, are connected to every realtor website in the country as well as internationally. It's a true "home buying information superhighway." All of this has emerged and come to fruition as the new norm in just the last 10 years. Therefore, do you really want to take the risk of going to battle with 1% or less of gross revenue allocated to what is now just as important as the land deal?

How are you going to stand out among a forest filled with trees— your competitors—and an abundance of information sources for home buyers? And good luck convincing the finance and equity guys that you should spend more than 1% of gross revenue to be better at marketing and assure that you hit your sales velocity and absorption goals.

So, what should you do? The answer is in assuring that you put as much thought into the "M" variable and figuring out a way to do it better, more efficiently, and in many cases proving that 1% is well invested and will get great results. Then it will be a no brainer to ask for 1.5% for even better and faster results. This means you need to build a proven lead generation program as well as an effective lead processing system in which your entire team (Marketing and online and onsite Sales) work in tandem. Your

Sales organization culture should be functioning so it can be relied on in the realm of a simple mathematical deduction:

Marketing Dollars In > Get Leads > Do Tours > Sales Out!

The holistic answer to building a proven home selling and lead generation program lies in becoming a multifaceted and efficient fisherman, which ultimately results in a conversion driven sales organization that firmly aligns Sales and Marketing. In other words, Marketing (aka fishing guides, the person who finds the fish) commits to generating the best quality leads they can, and Sales (aka anglers, the person reeling in the rod) commits to filtering and working those leads. Making the entire organization aligned in the commitment of working leads and converting them to buyers.

So, if you are a residential new home builder or developer, then you're in the right place, because this book was written just for you. You're about to learn how some of your most successful competitors are able to find more buyers and sell more homes to achieve their ROI goals. This is your marketing strategy playbook.

In short, you are about to discover how to "fish for home buyers" with the skill of a master fisherman whose secret weapon is an expert "fishing guide" who knows how to help builders find all of the home buyers they need, in the most effective way. You're going to learn the angling tips to help Sales reel them in. If you have the staff, you can do this on your own. If you don't, you'll learn what to expect from an agency managing the "M" variable.

If your first thought is that you already have a marketing program, or your company already does some marketing to sell your new home inventory or homesites, then this playbook is still for you. It's okay to do just "some" marketing, as long as you only plan on selling "some" homes. The days for passively promoting your developments and doing "some" marketing are far behind us. The competition for every single qualified buyer is fierce in most marketplaces, and the most effective and efficient ways to find and connect with qualified buyers is constantly evolving. Now more than ever. Who would have thought in the mid-2000s, when social media was first introduced that people would find homes and buy real estate through those channels?

I don't build homes or create developments for a living. But I do create blueprints. Not the kind that show your crew where every wall and outlet should be placed. I create blueprints to help builders and residential developers, like you, find the buyers you need, to make your projects a success.

In short, my team and I can help you find the buyers that want to buy your homes as fast and as cost efficiently as possible, so you can move on to the next opportunity. I have acquired my knowledge and subject matter expertise by serving builders and developers as a marketing partner for over 18 years (all being part of the evolution of the digital era in real estate).

Think of me and my team as expert "fishing guides" helping builders and developers fish for home buyers. That is, generating quality leads, converting those leads, and selling home inventories faster. Since 2002, my companies have generated over 8 million leads resulting in over $4 billion in home sales all over the U.S. and across the Americas. Over these past 15+ years, the most successful strategies to generate these leads has changed significantly and continues to evolve. As expert guides, we must be constantly on top of the most effective and available tactics and tools to deliver measurable and amazing results.

That's why I have decided to share what I've learned about generating and converting qualified leads for new home builders and developers. This is **The Marketing Strategy Playbook for Residential New Home Builders and Developers**. Whether you are the builder that believes in doing "some" marketing, traditional marketing, cutting-edge digital marketing, or some combination of each, I am about to open up my playbook to reveal the most effective ways to help you sell more homes, faster, and with accountable ROI. Even if you decide to continue using the same old marketing methods that you've always used, I'll show you how to yield better results with your "tried-and-true" methods.

In this business, the importance of a sales and marketing machine is how it generates product absorption and sales velocity that aligns with your ROI goals for every development deal you launch. The thing that matters most is if you can actually **sell your homes as quickly as you need to**. To do that you need buyers! And you are about to learn the best ways to "fish" for all of the buyers you need to make your projects a success. I'm about to show you the best places to fish, the best equipment to have with you, the best bait to use, how to reel in your bites, and how to cook them all the way to the closing table.

So, if you're ready to create a proven lead generating machine to find more buyers and sell more homes…let's get fishing!

"Don't mind me. I'm about to go fishing all lines in!"

Chapter 1
Fishing for Buyers
and Selling More Homes

*"We are in a digital age and
competition for your potential buyers
is fierce."*

Now that we're clear you're in the business of *selling* homes, the objective is to show you the best strategies, so you can find more buyers and quickly enough to achieve your financial targets.

I meet builders and developers all of the time that don't believe in advertising at all. They think that having Sales people do their own lead generation or relying on realtors to sell their homes is an effective plan. Yes, that is a plan—but a bad one, and one that seldom works anymore.

As I have already stated, we are in a digital age and competition for your potential buyers is fierce. If the success of your deal is dependent upon a Sales team that might not be as dedicated or as motivated as you think, you're leaving too much at risk. The same thing goes for realtors. With the choice of many developments, your inventory might not be a priority at all, especially if you are hard to find online or geographically. If you really want to take control of your deal, then you need more control over the promotion of your homes.

You need to have a system in place for more predictable lead generation, so you can also have more predictable sales.

I describe this process as fishing (for new home buyers) with the help of an expert guide and benefiting from years of experience, tested methods, and knowledge about the best bait, lures, equipment, and locations to find what you want. Sure, you can fish without an expert at your side. But your results won't be as good as they would be with the help of an expert.

The same thing goes for online advertising, email, outdoor media, TV, radio, social media, or even plain old newspaper and magazine ads. When you tap into the experience of an expert guide, you have a better chance of improving your results and getting the most return for every dollar you spend to market your homes. If you decide to try some of the newest and most exciting ways to really drive traffic to your communities, like geofencing and programmatic advertising, then having an expert to guide you through the most effective way is the only way to go.

Throughout this book, I will go deeper into the different marketing tools available to help you "fish for buyers" for your homes and communities. You might only choose to use a few of the available tools, or you might use each to some extent. My goal is to show you how to get the most out of every marketing dollar you have available to sell your homes quickly and move on to the next deal. What you'll soon discover is that even some of the "traditional" ways that new homes and developments are advertised in (such as print, outdoor media, radio, and TV) have evolved with the digital age. Meaning there are new ways to boost the old ways of advertising.

What Oceans Are Your Buyers In?

One of the ways I like to explain how to think of your prospective buyers and where to find them, is to use an ocean analogy. Your buyers are located in different "oceans" and if you want to lure in the number of prospects you need, then you need to "fish" in the all of those different oceans available to you. One "ocean" might be online search engines such as Google or listing websites such as New Home Source or Zillow. Another might be direct mail or radio ads. There are several oceans filled with potential buyers; the challenge is determining the best oceans to find fish for YOUR development. This where an expert is key to helping you find the best combination of marketing options that yield the best results.

Every ocean, just like in regular fishing, requires different tackle to be successful, which is influenced by the calendar and weather. To be successful in every ocean, you need expertise in every tactic, as each channel has its own set of nuances required to be successful.

It all starts with a comprehensive and integrative plan using multiple tactics. Each tactic or tool is like another fishing line in the water, working to drive predictable traffic (bites) to your community, so you can sell more homes. These tactics all work hand-in-hand to yield optimal results. When all lines are in, results can be five times higher than without.

In order to get the volume of leads you need to drive the required traffic to your communities, you might need to fish in several oceans. And you'll need an expert that knows what you can expect from each ocean and how to maximize your efforts there.

Whether you have a few lines in the water, or all lines in, you need a plan. Your efforts need to be tracked and your results and engagements need to be integrated into a CRM that fuels the efforts of your Sales team. When all of the pieces of your sales process are efficient, integrated, monitored, and optimized, you'll have the makings of your very own lead generation and home selling machine.

"I always bring my best fishing tackle and expert guide along."

Chapter 2
Your Content Assets
(Lures & Bait)

*"It's what gets 'em
and keeps 'em
in the sales funnel..."*

When you start fishing for prospective home buyers, every content piece your team develops to inspire and attract interest are the lures and bait that will fuel your home selling lead machine. Many underperforming developers fail to realize the importance of creating high quality content. They put all of their effort into building a beautiful development and then try to sell it with boring and unimaginative sketches and black and white images. That's not bait!

Even crazier is the situation where a builder gets in. They know there needs to be a marketing budget and spends it on ads to drive traffic. But the problem is they drive that traffic to a dead-end, boring online "brochure" that fails to inspire buyer interest or action.

Your content is a powerful component of your lead generation machine. It's what gets 'em and keeps 'em in the sales funnel as they explore your inventory and begin the sales process. The most successful home sellers are the ones that embrace the ideology that content is the bait needed to lure and engage prospects.

You will also need a communication strategy that differentiates the content you publish from the rest of the market. Without that, you are just doing what everyone else does, which is market your offer without addressing the emotional connection to the buyer.

It all starts with investing in great renderings of your homes, elevations, community amenities, floor plans, virtualization, video, outstanding selections of stock photography, and onsite photography of your products and model residents.

Exterior

Rendering

Floor Plan

Interior

Amenity

Lifestyle

Video

Virtual Reality

One key starting point is to have architectural images. Black and white images need to be converted into full color market renderings, floor plans, elevations, and images of what the community is going to look like when completed.

I can't overemphasize that images are very important and are the first things to attract interest in your development.

If your development is not completed enough for community photos, then use stock photography. You need to bring the lifestyle of the new community to life. This will help your prospective buyers get a sense of what it would feel like to live in your homes and will make a huge difference in your overall brand, tone, and message.

It's important to realize that you are not just competing against new home builders and communities, but the entire resale market as well. Most realtors prepare 40+ images, virtual tours, video, and staged homes to stay on par with what is standard on listing sites like Trulia and Zillow. You don't want to be outgunned.

It's imperative to use photo realistic renderings and relevant stock as well as virtual content to provide a virtual experience. Virtual reality is the latest technology that allows consumers to step into and experience a home through virtual simulation. It yields a powerful experience for the consumer and can drive consumer activity, preference, and purchases. Anything you can provide that enables your potential buyers to virtually enter your homes and experience the development will help to create a memorable adventure that can sell your homes. Providing a master plan of the community and a plat map will also engage potential buyers.

The possibilities are not limited to a virtual walk-through. Give prospects the opportunity to change wall colors or cabinet finishes through simulation. Providing a payment calculator is also helpful. When you give a potential buyer the opportunity to interact and customize, this is engagement that sells. This is actually becoming a standard. Therefore, not offering these options in your current or next projects will put your homes or developments in an inferior position.

Carefully prepared and selected images will do extra duty for advertising, your website, and third-party listing websites such as Trulia, Zillow, New Home Source, New Homes Directory, Homes.com, BuzzBuzzHome, and Privatecommunities.com. These images and assets will be invaluable in helping prospects begin to experience your homes. As more and more of your peers understand the importance and accept the value of visual content, having these assets to support marketing efforts will become the expected standard of buyers.

Your content includes your entire digital footprint, including your website, landing pages, Google Business page, online advertorials, YouTube content, social media posts, and high-quality SEO backlinks. Your search engine optimized articles and blog posts are also attraction magnets that will lure potential buyers into your sales funnel. This digital content now goes all the way into providing a customized experience through virtualization and online selection tools.

Blog Post

Facebook Page

YouTube Channel

Google Business

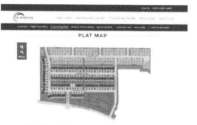

Online Interactive Plat Map

Sales Office Floor Plan Kiosk

Content also includes all of the features and technology your model homes offer, from sales slicks and onsite sales materials to interactive kiosks with features such as floor plans and plat maps. It includes assets like your print ads, print collateral, onsite sales materials, and community signage.

Your content needs to be fresh and engaging. It needs to be relevant to your target market. It needs to bring value, answer questions, and pique interest. It must also feature appealing visual images or video to attract more attention. It must be sharable with sharing options included. It needs to inspire action so that it encourages prospects to take the next step – make a call, click a link, sign up to be on your email list, or visit your development.

Investing in virtualization of home plans when in pre-sales, adding great photography and videos once the community has launched, and using great copy to articulate your story are all the foundation of putting together a digital model home that will generate the kind of engagement that gets potential buyers to take action and convert into home sales.

"An image is worth a thousand fish."

Chapter 3
Your Online Model

*"The goal is to open a virtual door
that the prospect can walk through
and engage with..."*

(Blackburn Communities Website Homepage)

Your online presence (yes, your website) is the most significant sales and marketing rep on your team that showcases your new home inventory and communities 24/7. Potential home buyers are internet savvy. Most start their own research online and when they find your website, you can either pre-sell them or you can push them away. In the next section, I'll show you how buyers find you. But right now, let's talk about what you have waiting for them when they do find you. Will your online presence say, "welcome home" or will it say, "we don't care"?

If you're going to create an online model and experience, then you should be prepared to do things professionally so that prospects are excited about visiting the development. That means investing in high-quality images along with a professionally designed and search optimized website. But that's just the beginning. Digital innovation such as virtual modeling and interactive floor plans go way beyond simple site optimization and pretty pictures. If you're serious about selling homes, then you don't want an online brochure—you need an online experience.

Building your builder/community website or landing page is very similar to building a new home. There is planning, design, decorating, process, and various tactical decisions in which critical details are analyzed and executed that ultimately impact the website's ability to become a lead generation machine while providing a world-class user experience.

With the launch of responsive web design tools, high performance builders who are serious about connecting with buyers and selling homes can now launch a more powerful website with amazing integration, analytics, and results. The goal is to open a virtual door that the prospect can walk through and engage with the virtual aspects of the development and model homes. They can't truly imagine themselves living there if you don't provide an opportunity for them to play with interactive features. You've got their attention; now you have to keep it so that they convince themselves that they have to contact you immediately and take the next step by visiting the development. In essence, you are starting the sales process the minute they find your online "selling machine."

Your digitally savvy and research-driven prospects want to discover curiosity-satisfying features like interactive floor plans and plat maps. They want to be able to save their favorites and learn more about your community through an available photo and video gallery. And most importantly, you'll know more about what matters to your prospects as their user behavior is monitored and tracked. Your prospects become fully engaged while your online model gathers intelligent buyer data to help your Sales team optimize follow up and sales activity.

The whole process becomes even more powerful, when all of this valuable prospect data is integrated with your CRM, so that your Sales team has real-time data to optimize the next phase of the sales process. A better user experience that reveals more useful data with interpreted analytics for your Sales team means you'll be able to find and qualify more buyers and sell more homes.

Getting this aspect of your selling machine right shouldn't be left to chance or to some poorly designed website. The most effective websites and web pages are carefully planned and strategized. User experience must be the driving focus on every single page. There are different pages or microsites that serve different purposes. And your web presence will likely evolve as your community projects evolve.

In many ways, creating the perfect online model mirrors the timing required for building a home, which means this online model can come in many shapes and sizes and require different production times. To clarify, a landing page or microsite—think of as a manufactured home/sales trailer often used for pre-sales—can be designed and built out in 2-4 weeks. The starter community or small builder website can take 3-4 months—like a production home. A larger, multi-community builder website, with different details on every page template and different desktop and mobile experiences, can take 6-12 months—just like phase one of a master-planned development. You can also have additional phases for websites of that nature when adding additional communities and content experiences—building out the rest of the phases and amenities.

There are a variety of customizable solutions available in the marketplace that can serve your needs whether you have a single-community development, a multi-community development, or are a local market, regional, or national builder. Online models will vary based on purpose, project, and business; such as a single-page landing page for list building or a whisper campaign, a website for a new community, a master-planned community website with builder information, or a corporate home builder website that includes every community that builder builds homes in.

Your websites and landing pages also need to be compatible across all devices your prospects will use to find you – desktop, tablet, and smartphone. The reality is that 60% of buyers are researching homes on their smartphone, so it is necessary to optimize the experience now beyond responsiveness (when a website automatically adjusts page layout and images, originally designed for desktop, to fit a tablet or mobile screen). The most successful lead generation marketers now invest the extra effort in figuring out the conversion science details for mobile, so their websites don't just "adjust" but have a seamless mobile design as well.

If you are starting any website project today, you should start with designing the mobile experience first. By 2020, we expect 75% of research for new homes and communities to be conducted via smartphone. This is the complete opposite of how it all started (designing for desktop and then mobile). This means you need to go beyond a simple reliance on responsive design technology. Responsive design can get you by, but responsive alone will not get you optimal results. You have to tweak mobile experience for swiping, fast load times, using thumb clicks for call-to-actions instead of a mouse, and finger stretching (pinching your fingers together on a mobile screen and spreading them apart to enlarge an image).

As discussed in the last chapter, the visual and copy assets that you put on website pages is also very important. Your website pages should include beautiful images, a site map, opportunities to customize a model online, and more. Your website needs to be easy to navigate and designed for engagement. It should inspire online registrations, click to calls, and provide driving directions to your community models.

All content such as images, video, copy, interactive features, and page design as well as search engine optimization should all be in alignment with the mechanical aspects of your website. Load time is now more critical than ever as buyers are impatient, and it will impact your presence on SERPs (search engine results pages).

Your online model can and will differentiate you from competing community developments. Having a fully functional and strategically designed online presence is no longer noteworthy or extraordinary. It is now common and expected in order to truly compete in the current home selling landscape.

"Now I don't even need to leave home to go fishing!"

Chapter 4
How Buyers Find You

*"Organic search results
deliver prospects at the perfect time,
when THEY are looking
for what YOU are offering."*

There are several ways potential buyers can find your website. Some website traffic is organic and some you pay for. In Chapter 5 I'll explain the best strategies for paying to get found. But for now, let's talk about the basics of getting found organically.

The goal of any search engine is to help people find the most relevant and credible websites or web pages with the exact information they were searching for. If you want search engines like Google, Bing, and Yahoo to interpret your online resources as a perfect match to what your potential clients are looking for, then you need to formulate your website and web pages to be found.

There is a notion that this organic traffic is essentially FREE. It's NOT! There is a science behind organic search success. It requires a significant amount of effort and search engine optimization (SEO) expertise to identify all of the elements needed to not only be found by search engines but delivered as a top of page search result on a SERP.

Yet, despite the fact that organic search is not exactly free and will require funds and resources, this is not the same as paying to get found discussed in the next chapter, and still requires priority in your marketing plan. The most important reason why organic search should be a priority in your marketing efforts, is that search engine organic traffic is the best traffic you can get. Organic search results deliver prospects at the perfect time, when THEY are looking for what YOU are offering. They will generally spend more time on your site, are already organized, and they are more-ready to take the next step. SERPs are some of the best waters to fish in, and organic search result leads are the best catches you can make. But if you go it alone and throw your line in without understanding the mechanics behind it, you might not catch anything at all.

Getting found organically by search engines starts with keyword research. Just as you would research keywords for paid advertising, you'll do the same for organic search planning. You need to know the most relevant keywords, their search volumes, and competition. Optimal keywords need to be in alignment with the design and content of your website. They need to be infused into the site map and integrated into the natural copy of your website.

Keywords Everywhere   GET FREE API KEY   CONTACT US   FAQ   NEWS   VIDEOS

Show 50 entries   Copy Excel CSV PDF Print   Search:

Keyword	Volume	CPC	Competition	Volume (US)	CPC (US)	Competition (US)
builders in mcallen tx	70	$0.39	0.09	70	$4.79	0.24
homes for sale in mcallen tx with pool	110	$0.86	0.58	110	$0.71	0.72
homes for sale mcallen tx	2,400	$1.21	0.48	2,400	$1.51	0.53
modern houses for sale in mcallen tx	10	$1.10	0.73	0	$0.00	0
new homes for sale mcallen tx	210	$2.10	0.8	210	$2.11	0.83
new homes in mcallen tx	90	$2.78	0.8	90	$2.78	0.7
tres lagos	2,900	$0.57	0.07	1,300	$1.15	0.12

Showing 1 to 7 of 7 entries   Previous 1 Next

Every website starts with keyword research first. This data and insight are then shared with the copywriting team so that all developed content is keyword optimized and keywords are imbedded in the content naturally. Copy must also include the proper outline following the MLA writing style with correct title text, headline text, image alt tags, title tags, and meta descriptions—also keyword optimized per SEO best practices. These formatting and content aspects all help search engines understand exactly what your website is about and allowing new home online researchers to find your website when they are, for example, searching "homes for sale in McAllen, TX". At the minimum it's recommended to have these aspects in place for proper search engine indexing.

Back in the early 2000s, companies were able to "game" search engines and use "keyword stuffing" or massive low value backlinks to appear like a perfect and top-of-page match. However, Google stays relevant in the search engine business by constantly altering their algorithms so that users receive the most relevant and credible results when they search. Therefore, Google now penalizes these shady tactics and will bury your sight so deeply in search results that no one would ever find it.

The only way to be rewarded with organic traffic is to follow SEO best practices, which generally require that:

1. You accurately and properly tag and describe your content. Title tags, meta descriptions, and quality content must be the standard.

2. You produce fresh and frequent high-quality content with relevant keywords naturally integrated into the copy. Proper citations and verbiage that say exactly what your content is about, such as "Homes for Sale in McAllen, TX," are important content components. Content done properly can be the "secret sauce" that gets you noticed by the search engines.

3. It is also beneficial for your content to be cited and linked to (aka backlinks) by credible industry sites. Some low hanging fruit for builders might be to ask suppliers, vendors, and trade partners that you do business with to link back to your own web pages from their website. These backlinks must be cultivated and developed. Press releases, media articles, and links from ad sites like Trulia or Zillow can also help to boost your credibility ranking with search engines.

4.

(https://www.rgvnewhomesguide.com/tres-lagos-grand-opening/)

5. Social media pages and activity (posts, comments, and reviews) are now part of Google's algorithm that help with where your website ranks in search results. Load time is also critical. It requires optimizing code and compressing images—something that never stops if you are expanding content. Social media back linking to pages that have a lot of engagement are now just as important to boosting SERP ranking as tag work.

6. Your website must also feature technical components that make it easier for search engines to index your web pages. This means your pages must be well-coded for search engines to easily read and "crawl" your content. Equally as important is how good the mobile experience of your website is and load times. Expect these elements to become more and more important going into the 2020 decade.

(xml sitemap)

First and foremost, you should have a main website for your company brand name. Since it can take several months to be properly indexed by the search engines, the additional single-community websites, microsites, and landing pages that you optimize may depend upon how much time you expect to be developing and marketing homes in a community. The key is to realize the tremendous value in developing your online content assets for search engine optimization. This is how you will have the best opportunity to lure the best available fish into your net.

"I use Google to tell me where to fish."

Chapter 5
Paying to Get Found

"The reality is that PPC
is the equivalent of day trading
on Wall Street."

In the last chapter, I explained why organic traffic from search engines is so valuable – it connects you to the best fish in the ocean, buyers who are actually looking and ready to buy. Now, I want you to know why paying to get found is also a very important part of any marketing campaign. In fact, paid traffic or pay per click (PPC) also known as Search Engine Marketing (SEM), is one of the top three sources for driving traffic to your developments—the other two being organic searches and email.

This is one of the few channels where you can be found for thousands of keyword searches within 24 hours of launching a campaign and is typically the starting place for inexperienced firms starting to do digital marketing for their homes and communities. Depending on how targeted you make your keywords, SEM captures top of the sales funnel leads by buying broad market-based keywords such as "new homes for sale in Houston," (Houston being a large Texas DMA), to middle of the funnel leads that search for "new homes for sale in Katy, TX," (Katy being a particular city near Houston), and bottom of the funnel leads that are searching for a specific builder in a specific community, like "Saratoga Homes for sale in the Woodlands."

Back in the early 2000s, Google, in its early stages of its path towards search engine dominance and search engine monetization, unveiled its game changer. Google launched AdWords, now just called Google Ads, which was the search engine's keyword-based search engine advertising program. What started with just 350 advertising customers, now delivers keyword-based results for over tens of millions of businesses.

Initially, some marketers and businesses misperceived that getting paid to be found wasn't the most efficient or glorious way to find customers. Prevailing thought was that Google search results should be organic and free. Of course, we are now light years ahead in the evolution of the science behind paid search. Those who are now awake to the potential and value of Google Ads have fully embraced paid search traffic. PPC ads have the ability to drive consistent and qualified traffic straight to your home builder website. Google Ads, and other paid search engine traffic, is a key component to any marketing plan primarily because it has become the starting point for buyers researching their new home options and starting the buying process.

Another huge area for false assumptions is that buying traffic is a no-brainer. Some think that you can just open a Google Ads account, pick a couple of keywords, write a few ads, and hit GO on a campaign. This misunderstanding has been a contributing factor in the cost inflation of running paid search campaigns. But just as there is a science behind organic search, there are also optimization strategies behind paid search as well.

There could be thousands of keywords relevant to your business. A well-administered SEM campaign can help you avoid the costly learning curve of figuring out what works to get found and what doesn't. There are actually three key factors that must be in alignment for maximum effectiveness with a paid search or PPC campaign.

1. Choosing/targeting relevant keywords.
2. Creating the right ads to trigger interest.
3. Deliver traffic to the best content and best landing page experience that engages prospects.

Your Google quality score will also have an impact on the effectiveness of your campaigns. How well you match these three things and how you administer your bidding is what drives the quality score.

The reality is that PPC is the equivalent of day trading on Wall Street. Your search engine console is an auction that bids on keywords. It's important to stay on top of Google's constant tweaking to its ads console and ad requirements and consistently be making adjustments or risk getting exposed to changes that can be costly and diminish results.

So, at the end of the day, how do you make sure you're choosing the right keywords to bid on, designing the right ads to display, and creating the best landing page content to convert your traffic? If you're going to fish for prospects with paid traffic, you really need a fishing guide to do this the right way. You need someone who is "in the know" about all of the important insights, and never stops optimizing. Your guide will know how to vary keywords, optimize landing pages, and tweak your ads to improve results.

However, hiring any marketing agency to manage your PPC

marketing isn't enough. You need a marketing manager that specializes in the home building industry, in your area. Hiring a manager that knows your industry and market can go a long way to save you from wasting money on ineffective ads, while improving your return on investment. You are better off hiring a firm that specializes in real estate and preferably has knowledge of your market region, rather than using a traditional marketing agency or even worse your cable provider or media publisher to manage your PPC. This means you won't start from scratch. Instead you benefit from the experience of the firm that knows these waters and your niche.

(Negative Keyword List)

An experienced guide has already tested hundreds of keywords and has blacklisted keywords that would be a waste of money to bid on—your negative keyword list. You can burn a lot of money on experimentation, and you also need to know what search engines to use for your paid traffic. Back in 2000, Yahoo controlled 80% of search traffic, MSN was in second, and Google was a smaller 3rd place influence. By 2012, Google had achieved a dominating 85% market share, with Yahoo holding onto 10% and MSN barely maintaining 5%.

Today, due to some strategic planning by Microsoft putting their default browser on new Windows-based computers, Bing (formerly known as MSN) was about to recover 20% share of the search market. This means that even if the bulk of your traffic buys are on Google, there may be a possibility of keyword dominance with a portion of your budget directed to Microsoft's Bing. Bing traffic could include younger new computer buyers who could also fit the first-time home buyer demographic. The Bing factor can also influence the "older generation" that does not realize they are not even using Google as a search engine because Bing is their default page when opening a browser.

If you decide to fish for home buyers in the paid-traffic ocean, you can spend as little as $500/month just to buy your brand keywords, such as your specific markets or community name, or you can spend upwards of $10,000/month like some of the larger regional builders. This is the staple of every marketing program because it makes you relevant right away, and depending on the keyword strategy, you'll be able to find buyers in all stages of the buying cycle. Google should be the priority, as it has the largest market share by far, but Bing is a nice complement that requires minimal investment to capture, in most cases, 100% impression share with as little as $500/month.

One factor to note if you are going fishing in this ocean, is your bait needs to actually hook 'em. I.e. a well optimized landing page that generates form registrations, calls, and driving direction clicks to your model homes and sales centers. Also, do not overlook the remarketing campaigns that Google offers that go hand-in-hand with search. You need to have great digital banners that integrate with your landing page communication strategy.

The key takeaways here are that paid traffic from search engines, is one of the top three oceans to fish in for home buyers. But just like organic traffic, there is a science to doing this the right way, which means you need a fishing guide that knows the waters, giving you the benefit of your guide's experience and prior experimentation. Even more important is the need to work with a guide that specializes in your specific business and location.

"I'm not catching any bass…"
"That's because there aren't any bass in these waters. I think you asked the wrong guide."

Chapter 6
Email Marketing Strategies

*"50% of consumers
check their email
at least 10 times a day."*

Email marketing is an important piece of the residential new home builder and developer marketing strategy playbook. Email continues to be the number one, most frequently used, and cost-effective communication channel for sending marketing messages. Especially, to re-engage with potential buyers and realtors that have already opted-in.

There are over 250 million email users in the U.S. alone, and this number is expected to rise by a minimum of 15% annually. Consumers in the 33 to 45-year old age group subscribe to 15 email marketing offers on average, and approximately 50% of consumers check their email at least 10 times a day. Even millennials, still utilize email as a form of connecting and communicating.

The key to successfully implementing an email marketing campaign is to first be clear on the specific purpose of your emails and your target audiences. There are different types of home builder and developer email campaigns and each message you send must be customized to specifically appeal to and address the goal of your campaign and the interests of the recipients. With a few exceptions, your emails will typically fit into two categories—your emails will either be an attempt to get new prospects or to reengage your current list of prospects.

Types of emails include:

- **Opt-in List Emails** - These are messages to potential buyers that have already given you permission to communicate with them. They have already expressed interest in one or more of your developments. Messages to this group might be to promote an event, offer a call to action such as Download New Floor plan, or to inspire reengagement. These are known as event-based driven deployments of emails, also known as batch and blasts. Generally, your opt-in list should yield 18%-25% open rates. However, filtering your list by deployment purposes, community, and how long ago they opted in, is how you will get these optimal open and engagement rates. If you don't, expect to get 10% or lower as people filter more and more email, as well as email service providers. As a gauge for filtering out buyers, expect primary home buyers to be in the market for up to 12 months and active adults to be in the market for 4 years. More details ahead.

(Reengagement Email)

- **Realtor Emails** – These might be a single, broad-based message to the entire realtor association list to promote a specific event or new development announcement. They could also be more customized messages to a smaller but more engaged list of your prime realtor contacts. Your prime realtor list includes realtors who have engaged with your content and have brought you buyers. This is a B2B referral partner communication.

  What is important is customization so that your message speaks to your specific recipients. What you promote to a broad membership list isn't the same thing you would send to realtors that you already have a working relationship or quality connection with. If your prime realtor contact list is well managed and messages are sent from a good IP, you can probably expect a 15-25% average open rate. Messages that are sent to a broader, entire Realtor Association list will most likely yield a 2-10% open rate.

  Builders and developers should segment their realtor lists by the following: entire market, realtors that specialize in the part of the town the community is in, realtors that have referred home buyers, and those that have opted-in directly. Each one of these will have a different overall level of engagement, giving you options for developing emails for quality versus volume as well as broad versus more intimate.

- **Marketing Automation Driven Emails, (aka Drip Campaigns)** – These are automated, timed, one-to-one marketing messages tailored to a specific prospect for a specific campaign. An "action" by an individual (e.g. request to receive floor plans) will launch a series of pre-planned communications to progressively engage and encourage the recipient to transition toward a specific and more significant call to action. After planning and setting up your message sequence with an autoresponder for every action taken, each individual recipient will receive a continuous flow of messages after they initiate the first trigger or "action".

Drips

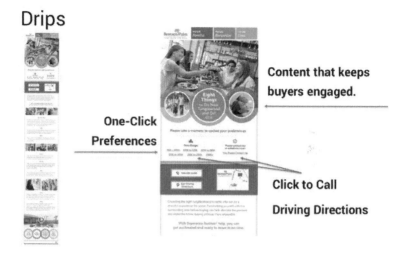

Drip campaigns also allow you to stay in front of potential buyers until they are ready to take action and make a purchase. We generally recommend that 6 months of content is developed and scheduled for prospects who enter your drip campaign funnel. Drip campaign content should be relevant to the buyer and specific to the community of interest. It can provide nuggets of information about the community, describe decoration options, feature amenities, showcase floor plans, and provide other tools and resources to help your prospect make an informed decision.

Drip content can be delivered as full creative emails as well as text-only messages. The best practice is to combine both. Ideally, your content strategy will match the buyer's journey. Marketing automation tools allow for the automated delivery of content based on predetermined rules and actions. The latest innovations in email marketing enable the delivery of persona-based or product-based content from gathering consumer data and applying it to a buyer's profile—sending specific content pieces that matches the criteria.

Persona-based emails, content that is highly personalized and relevant to a person's persona and buyer preferences, are highly effective. These emails are driven by buyer actions and buyer attributes captured in a registration form online or onsite, time on specific web pages, or information a sales professional has captured and entered into a CRM that triggers the delivery of persona content.

- **Third-Party Emails** – These emails are prospecting opportunities used to capture new contacts and potential buyers by marketing to third-party lists that are in alignment with your target market. An example of this would be your local newspaper's subscriber list. There are thousands of third-party lists available.

Too many times, I have seen builder marketing campaigns that use the same email messaging for all recipients. This is a mistake and will significantly reduce the effectiveness of your efforts. If you're going to fish for home buyers in email waters, then this too should be optimized, customized, and strategically designed to achieve the highest ROI.

There are five distinct strategies or fundamentals that are most important for an email campaign to be effective. However, success largely lies in the technical component, which every day is more and more complex due to the continuing surge of worldwide delivery and consumption of electronic mail.

1. List Quality

This depends on how engaged an email list is with your brand and developments. The best quality list is the list of potential buyers that have requested information about your homes and offerings and have given you permission to send them marketing messages. These are people that have already responded to your content or clicked a call-to-action and are your warm to hot buyer prospects. The least responsive and lowest quality lists to market to are third-party lists. Nevertheless, these less responsive email marketing opportunities are important to fish for new prospects and convert them to the list of prospects that have given you permission to send them more marketing messages.

2. List Management

List management is another crucial component when it comes to best practices of email marketing. Generally, in marketing circles the belief is that bigger lists are better. However, building a huge list without pruning it can cause consequences that will hinder your email campaign success.

This is one of the hardest realities to deal with in the evolution of Internet Service Providers (ISP) filtering emails. Marketing to a huge list of 10K email addresses, accumulated in the past 6 years, used to be a great asset. However, sending to all, if there is no engagement, can now be counter-productive as sending to unengaged users typically results in auto-filtering to junk, which can increase a potential new buyer's likelihood of getting your emails in the junk box vs. the inbox. Today, the best practice is to mail to contacts that have opted-in or registered onsite within the last 12 months or are actively engaged in opening your marketing emails. This applies to buyers and realtors.

As you continue to market your new developments, you might start to accumulate thousands of opt-in prospects. However, with your primary prospect email list, there are some very important reasons to actively manage and "clean" your list. The reality is that most buyers are in the market for only about one year. Once they have made a purchase, they will largely ignore your marketing messages—even if they eventually purchased one of your homes. Due to email delivery algorithms, this dismissal of your emails by prospects who are no longer in the market, can and will affect your sender reputation. This can cause your messages to appear as spam for all prospects and not just the ones who are unengaged, reducing your delivery rates and campaign success.

Generally, it's recommended that there be a cut-off for how long a prospect stays on your list without any engagement. If a prospect has been inactive for 12 months, they should be purged from your email list. They have likely already purchased a home or are no longer in the market.

3. Subject Lines and Sender Reputation

Subject lines, and even sender names, will also impact your campaign's deliverability and open rates. However, subject lines and IP sender reputation (not to be confused with sender name) are two totally separate things. Once an email makes it to the inbox, besides the sender name, a subject line is the most important factor in determining if a message is opened. Aside from enticing copy, it encounters spam tools that trigger filtering. There are 100s of free subject line testing tools that help you assess how likely your audience will be to open your message and how likely it will be filtered as spam. This is a must-do step for any serious marketer.

Sender reputation is the most important behind the scenes factor. ISPs and blacklists around the world keep sender scores for every IP address that tries to deliver mail to their infrastructure. They determine reputation on quality of delivery to your lists based on number of bounces, complaints, spam traps, and frequency. Typically, a marketer controls the email list, but as it regards to IPs and sender reputation, that is managed by the email service provider whether it's the email service that comes with your CRM, a third-party mailing service such as Constant Contact or Mailchimp, or your own in-house solution. They all have inherent pros and cons in regard to reputation and what they will or won't let you do with lists. If you are a serious mailer, this is an area you should understand and stay informed on—especially, if you are having challenges.

This is another important reason to work with a firm that specializes in your niche. You can waste a lot of your marketing budget on testing subject lines to discover what words and phrases yield the best click-through rates, when an experienced firm already knows how to avoid spam words and elude aggressive spam filters. Your sender reputation and IP address will also influence whether or not your marketing messages survive the journey into a prospect's inbox.

4. Content

Even if you have the best list, an intriguing subject line, and 100% deliverability, none of that matters if your prospects click-through and encounter ineffective and poorly-planned content. From the design of your email message to your strategically placed calls-to-actions, your content is the driving force to engage and reengage your prospects and push them through your sales funnel. There is even a science on perfect content structure with best practices for image to text ratios. More on this in a bit.

5. Timing

Timing is critical. Every inbox can quickly get filled with an enormous amount of distractions. Your message has the best chance of being seen if delivered during parts of the day when people are most likely to check their email. People generally have free time to check their email right after breakfast, lunch, and dinner. This makes 9-11 am, 2- 4 pm, and to a lesser degree 7-10 pm the most effective delivery time windows. Weekends have also re-emerged as a great time for home buyer and realtor emails, especially if delivered 8-10 am on Saturday and Sunday mornings. People have less clutter in their inboxes and less distractions outside of the inbox meaning more discretionary time to read and interact with your content.

Content Continued...

The quality, value, and design of your content will directly impact the effectiveness of your email marketing efforts. There are several aspects and considerations that must be built into your content pieces, otherwise your efforts and investment could be wasted. Some of the top email content best practices include:

- Including consistent branding and logos
- Engaging headlines
- Accolades/credibility features
- Prominent calls-to-actions that are short and sweet and provide multiple action opportunities
- Engagement opportunities for buyers to click, such as
    - Floor plans that are easy to read and linked to your website, especially for mobile users
    - Opt-in and download e-brochures
    - Linked location maps
    - Click-to-calls
    - Driving directions
    - Schedule an appointment/tour
    - Follow social channels
    - List of or link to available inventory
    - Questions to gauge where they are in the process, product preferences, etc.
    - Invite to launch events/RSVPs
- General one-click preferences
- Properly sized renderings that are not too oversized that they obstruct quick notice of primary call-to-actions
- Model home or community address, phone number, and pricing

COMMUNITY MAPS

BUYER PREFERENCES

CLICK-THROUGHS TO NEIGHBORHOODS

(Developer Reengagement Email)

HOMES AVAILABLE NOW · FROM THE $440S

Make your move to Fronterra
at Westpointe.

When you choose a new home at Fronterra at Westpointe, the only thing you leave behind is city taxes! This family-friendly community is served by an excellent school district. And it's just a short drive to several major employers, San Antonio International Airport, and first-class shopping and dining.

Take a look at these beautiful homes available for immediate move-in, all located in the community's exclusive gated section.

CLICK TO CALL & DIRECTIONS

AVAILABLE INVENTORY

BUYER PREFERENCES

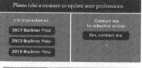

If having more to spend on the activities or people you love appeals to you, visit Fronterra at Westpointe and tour these exquisite homes. Sitterle Homes has won multiple awards for design, construction, and customer service. We'd be honored to be your builder!

(Builder Reengagement Email)

The key take-away for this chapter is that email marketing can, with the click of a button, drive buyers to your development and nudge them to continue their journey through your sales funnel. These are waters that will yield you plenty of qualified fish to buy your inventory. However, you can also waste a lot of marketing budget and effort if you attempt email without a marketing guide that knows how to map out a campaign that gets delivered, gets seen, and inspires action.

Start with the end in mind. What action do you want your audience to take when they consume your content? Plan your content strategy around that. Avoid the wall of text. Bullets, call outs, and images that engage are always going to be easier to digest and more likely to influence engagement.

"I never catch the same fish with the same bait."

Chapter 7
Social Media Strategies

"The results speak for themselves."

Social media provides two mechanisms to help you boost new home sales. In addition to social media page management, there are multiple opportunities to deliver paid advertising to highly targeted audiences. Of course, there are also various ways to optimize how you use social media to yield better conversions and there are best practices that will help you to improve the value you can create with your social presence.

SmartTouch Interactive
April 13, 2018 at 6:26pm · 🌐

Raise brand awareness through social media partners, video content, and social media contest & events.

👍 Like   💬 Comment   ➦ Share

Why Social Media?

Social media improves your marketing efforts in multiple ways, including:

- Raising brand awareness
- Cultivating brand affinity

- Building new audiences, creating a following, and growing existing audiences
- Increasing web traffic to your websites and landing pages
- Showcasing and validating the joys of home buying and designing
- Driving more leads with targeted advertising
- Increasing organic search traffic by combining the significance of social proof with SEO efforts to enhance value with search engine algorithms

As you can imagine, these are all great reasons to devote a portion of your marketing budget to build and manage your social media presence. And as with all of your marketing options, there are ways to get the most out of every dollar spent on social media. These platforms all offer their own paid advertising options to highly targeted profiles or lookalike lists.

First, let's talk about paid promotions on Facebook and then strategies for social media page management across platforms.

Facebook Targeting & Lookalike Lists

Facebook provides a dynamic platform for highly targeted advertising. Using Facebook Audiences, people can be identified and screened by their demographics, interests, and behaviors. These audiences can be further defined by their activity such as website visits and video views. And they can be pre-qualified by creating lookalike lists, which are based on similarities to your current customers and prospects. Thus, we can now build audiences that demonstrate an interest before we put ads in front of them, ultimately generating a better lead based on prior interests. This allows you to create a highly targeted funnel and increase lead quality.

The Secret Sauce to Facebook Paid Advertising

Over time, we have been able to identify some optimal strategies to maximize the value of social media marketing. Probably about a year and a half ago, Facebook was a top source for lead generation but not a top source for tours and home sales. Our challenge was identifying ways to improve the quality of leads generated through Facebook ads. We were able to achieve some significant improvements by providing customer match and lookalike lists. But the real "secret sauce" was when we started to build audiences that had demonstrated prior intent.

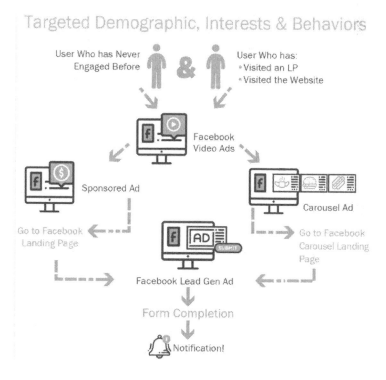

We would start with audiences that met all of our demographic, interest, and behavior parameters. Then we applied our match/lookalike screening factors. And finally, we further screened by those who took the time to watch at least 50% of our videos. Only then would a prospect truly start the Facebook

Audience Funnel that lead through the screening process of landing page form submissions, lead gen submissions, and becoming a qualified lead. The results speak for themselves. We had "cracked the code" to developing a more qualified prospect. While lead volume is lower, the leads generated are much better. This strategy uses all of the different types of new generation paid advertising available on Facebook, including video, Carousel, Newsfeed/Sponsored, Canvas, and Lead Gen ads.

Essentially, Facebook Audiences is a great source for generating home buyer leads. There are multiple campaign types available to accomplish multiple goals. And most importantly, more targeted ads mean putting ads in front of the right people and higher quality leads.

Social Media Page Management

In addition to Facebook, there are other social media channels that can boost the impact of your marketing efforts, including Twitter, Instagram (now a part of Facebook), Pinterest, and probably most importantly, the emergence of Google My Business. Google My Business controls business listings on Google and is one of the most important pages to keep up to date, as in many cases, 50% of your brand's Google traffic is coming through your business listings.

- **Twitter**: Twitter is a great way to provide up-to-date information on listings, homes recently sold, and other types of community event news. It helps to engage and update followers.

- **Instagram**: Instagram helps to increase media reach and to increase engagement with followers in a more intimate, visually-driven way.

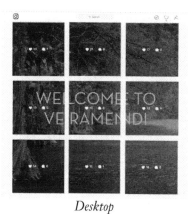

Desktop

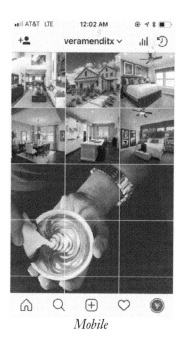

Mobile

- **Pinterest**: Pinterest is an amazing platform for posting linked and sharable content. Each image posted can refer traffic back to your website. Sharable content can include home images and community features. Boards can be created to showcase and share content about a community. You can also collaborate with influencers to create boards featuring images that will trigger clicks and drive traffic to your landing pages.

Social media page and post management can also help raise brand awareness and increase buyer interest in your communities. You can use social media channels to:

- Reach out and connect with social media partners
- Share video assets to promote your communities
- Showcase available inventory
- Announce home sales
- Feature pictures of buyers to bridge connections to your buyers' circles of influence and friends
- Post updates about your communities

- Promote open house events and more
- Engage and update your followers
- Reach out and engage with local community interest groups or schools
- Generate reviews
- Promote engagement activities such as contests and events

Contests and Events

Featuring and sharing contests and events has proven to be a highly effective activity for connecting and engaging with potential buyers. It helps to build and maintain your brand and online presence. You can leverage the promotion of these activities to increase followers and engagement. It helps to activate your followers to help you grow your prospect list, grow your brand, and increase home sales.

Social media marketing, while not the most important element of your marketing strategy, can still play a significant role in boosting your other advertising activities and generating additional highly-qualified leads.

"Fish are social creatures too."

Chapter 8
Listing Websites -
Optimization Strategies

*"The goal here is not
to try to out rank these destination sites,
but to work with them..."*

Do a quick Google search for, "new homes _____" and insert the city where your community or development is located. The first thing you will notice is that the top organic results are usually dominated by top listing websites such as Trulia.com, Zillow.com, NewHomeSource.com, NewHomesDirectory.com, Realtor.com, Homes.com, BuildersUpdate.com, Redfin.com, and a handful of others. These heavy-hitter websites tend to dominate keyword rankings for the most valuable and direct searches in most markets. Because of this, they are the most popular destination sites where home buyers begin their search.

The goal here is not to try to outrank these destination sites, but to work with them and to have a presence on them. There are several opportunities for paid advertising on these websites with preferred and promoted listings and companion ads near your featured listings.

The key to leveraging these websites is to integrate your CRM so that leads are captured in the CRM and workflows are triggered to notify your Sales team to take action. We want leads to engage with us by calling, registering, and in many cases, clicking on driving directions to model homes and communities.

The leads generated from listing websites are high-intent prospects. There's really only one reason to go to these sites and that's because you're in the market and looking to buy. In most cases this is where the customer journey begins. This is where buyers can learn about different communities and do their initial research. It is common for potential buyers to visit as many as 10 websites BEFORE they even get into the car. And they may even opt to not fill out the lead form but do their research and just show up at your model home. These are high-value leads, so you need to have a presence on these websites, and again, work with them.

One key thing to add is that these websites need to be updated with the richest content you have (video, virtual tours, floor plans, images, and renderings). The better the content, the more leads you'll get. If you're rolling with old school black and white rendering, save your money. Remember when it comes to listing websites you are competing for a street address and not just against other new home builders and communities, but resales which typically feature around 30 WOW shots, virtual tours, drone and in-house video.

Content is KING!

Best practices for optimizing your ROI on these websites is to have high-quality assets to feature. This means lots of great home images, a virtual tour, engaging videos, and access to floor plans. Generally, the more high-quality images available, the better the ad conversion. And the more listings and more communities you have to choose from, the better the response rates.

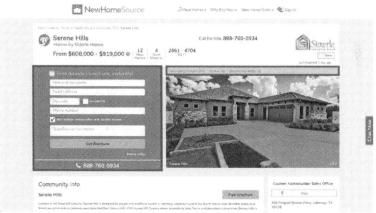

(Example includes 17 photos, 1 video, 2 community maps, and a free floor plans brochure.)

Your best chance at a successful marketing campaign is to be in all of the places where you can engage with potential buyers. This is essentially what I mean by, "All Lines In." You need to have all of your lines in the water using all of the available tools to connect with prospects, and you need to have those lines in all of the places (oceans) where your buyers could be. Listing websites are where people who want to buy, typically start their search. If you don't want them to start their search without you, then you need to have a presence on these high-buyer-intent websites.

"High-Quality Content: the best bait out there."

Chapter 9
Display Advertising
& Remarketing

"Pay for actions
vs views."

Third-party websites present an opportunity for you to be seen on high traffic sites with featured ad feeds. Despite being disruptive advertising, this exposure can yield significant returns connecting you to potential and interested buyers. These websites dominate search results, so it's important to have an appearance in their feeds that can also be amplified with display advertising.

However, you can also buy local media, entertainment, and national news sites from Google Display Network and pay pennies instead of $1000s of dollars on impressions (known as CPM or cost per impression ads). Instead, you will only pay per click (PPC) for traffic.

To further explain the key differentiator that will provide results in the most cost-efficient manner—if you were to directly secure advertising on these listing sites, you would be purchasing advertising on a CPM scale. This means you pay for views vs. action. With disruptive ads this could be very costly and ineffective. Paying on a PPC scale means you only pay when someone clicks your ad and not just if they see it.

Two fundamental ways we work with clients to provide critical presence on these web properties while maintaining optimal effectiveness is with Google display ads and remarketing ads. First, let's cover the reason for Google. By using Google's Display Network, we can have an advertising presence on national and high-value local websites that are specific to our target keywords. However, instead of paying for ads on a CPM basis, we would be buying PPC ads. In this way, we would only pay for viewers who had some interest, enough to click for more information and to connect to a landing page. We want to pay for action vs. views.

Buying display advertising through Google's network allows you to purchase PPC style and be on 100s of important websites relevant to your brand and target buyer. Display ads are great for generating awareness in your local market and building a pre-launch blitz but not as effective as a straight-up lead gen tactics. So, typically, you can get a lot of website visits and ad impressions for as little as $500/month.

Remarketing versus display becomes a factor when it comes to brand awareness. We aim to further optimize our banner ad strategy by making sure that the web visitors that see our ads in the first place are the best possible prospects we can target. We achieve this with remarketing ads. This allows our clients to promote ads to prospects that have already visited one of their websites or landing pages. I.e. if a prospect has visited a landing page for a development and leaves without taking action, then the next time they are checking their local news site, they could see a remarketing ad for the same development. This familiar content refreshes their interest in your offer and drives traffic back to your website.

The remarketing experience drives dramatically higher conversion rates and allows you to re-engage prospects who initially expressed some interest. These are typically better-quality leads since they, by taking action a second time, are essentially re-affirming their interest in your offer. This strategic audience building is another key component to a comprehensive plan to sell more homes, faster.

"I feel like I've seen you somewhere before..."

Chapter 10
Geofencing -
The Game Changer

"… the most revolutionary
advertising tactic I've come across
in the last 18 years of digital marketing."

Most of the ways a builder can connect with buyers today are the same ways it has been done for decades. Of course, internet technology has altered the home selling landscape with websites, landing pages, and email. But there is a more recent technological innovation that is truly a marketing game changer - geofencing. I believe geofencing is the most revolutionary advertising tactic I've come across in the last 18 years of digital marketing.

Geofencing

Geofencing is location-based marketing. The best way to describe a geofence is like a virtual fence around a specific location. The geofence can detect when someone enters and leaves the perimeter or predefined geo-territory. Once detected, a person's presence can trigger an alert or action such as a notice to the party tracking the area and/or send a message to a visitor's mobile phone. The mobile device is the tool that enables people to be tracked and messaged. Mobile devices can be tracked using cellular data, bluetooth beacons, GPS, WiFi, or RFID (radio-frequency identification).

Geofencing can also be used to track behavior (such as how long a person visits your store) or to provide relevant messaging and content to visitors in or near your business (such as a coupon to get them to visit to your store). You might even get a coupon (or pitch) from a nearby competitor to draw you away from a business and toward their product. Some other interesting applications include smart appliances and business equipment tracking. One interesting situation might be a notice from your refrigerator telling you that you need to get more milk as you pass a grocery store. Geofencing can also be used to adjust temperature or secure access as people come in and leave a home or business.

SmartTouch® Geo

We initially tried geofencing about 4 years ago with disappointing results. We were paying per impression with low click-through rates and unimpressive results for a VIP client that was open to experimenting, a McWhinney development called The Lakes at Centerra located in Loveland, Colorado, led by Kim Perry VP of Community Design and Neighborhood Development.

After further analysis and strategic changes, we launched SmartTouch® Geo in 2017. SmartTouch® Geo is breakthrough geofencing technology built specifically for residential home builders and developers.

The way home buyer geofencing is executed is the difference maker. This cutting-edge marketing approach can take your location targeting campaigns to the next level with better conversion rates and ROI.

Simply put, this technology can get people to change their behavior.

SmartTouch® Geo delivers high-intent prospects to your

developments in 5 easy steps: A key attribute to its success are the ads. The more intent driven, the better.

We have clients that have the address of the model home on the ad with a click that gets you immediately to a landing page with driving directions. Or, in some cases, the ad highlights features that an alternate competitor community or builder may not have.

These often work best...messages developed by location. In addition, letting Sales know what and who you are targeting is key, so they can record tours and tie back which buyers came from geofence ads. Quite often asking the simple question, "Hi, are you home shopping today?" will get a buyer to disclose what other communities they have toured.

Geofencing is the most cost-effective marketing tactic that drives immediate qualified buyers. At the same time, for marketers, it is one that can be controversial as you have to overcome skepticism about it actually working. I myself actually got geofenced while buying a vehicle in December 2017. I was shopping Acura and Infiniti for a high-tech featured, smaller SUV with an alternate 3rd row seat.

As I left the Acura dealership, I checked my phone and got an ad for Toyota of Cedar Park's year end sale with 0% interest and $2k off MSRP. I walked out with a 2018 Toyota Highlander and saved $20K while getting all the technology I wanted.

Here's how we employ SmartTouch® Geo:

1. First, we identify the various target locations where your best prospects might be located. This could be local businesses, a real estate office, apartment complexes, or a competitor's model home.

2. The next step is to capture the mobile device ID of the people that enter these target zones (the geofenced area).

3. Then we deliver our mobile ads to the geo-located shoppers, sending them to various conversion zones. Multiple target and conversion zones can be created.

4. Shoppers are then tracked back to conversions zones (your developments and model homes) to determine how many shoppers converted to tours.

5. The result is more bottom of the funnel buyers, more tours, and more sales.

The buyer must have an app on their mobile device with enabled location services. SmartTouch® Geo uses over 30 exchanges to syndicate, which covers over 95% of ad slots on the web/mobile apps available inside of our network.

Relevancy is also a critical component. We take great care in customizing the message to the target audience. For renters, we might promote cost of rent vs. monthly mortgage payments for affordable developments. We might provide driving directions. We might target a doctors' parking lot for high-end developments. We could also target shoppers who are at your competitor's model home and get them to change their plans and behavior, so they leave that model home and come to visit your development.

It is not a huge click driver. People who are on their phone have very little attention span. However, it will influence behavior, especially for people that are in the decision comparison mode. Also, it's not limited to model homes. Our clients have had great results geofencing doctor parking lots at hospitals, major employer parking lot, fitness centers, an entire Air Force base, a concert, etc. It can become very relevant especially if you can remarket once you capture mobile phone IDs. But in most cases, the most effective engagement happens right away.

As you can imagine this provides a powerful opportunity to connect with people who are perfectly geo-positioned to take action. These aren't just shoppers, these are buyers. Especially if they are at a model home. They are not just starting their new home search; they are getting ready to purchase. So, these buyers are perfect targets to draw toward your model home. The bottom-line is that the average cost per unit of traffic is less than $50 when utilizing geofences and geofence ads.

Geofencing delivers more buyer traffic to your properties and that inevitably sells more homes. Because of this, I recommend it as a staple in every marketing program. And if you can only spend on one marketing tactic – it must be geofencing. Don't get me wrong, you can't geofence your entire town. This game changing "lure" is impression-based and today it's driven via CPM. So, the more impressions you serve the more costly it gets. That's why smaller, highly-targeted geofences around competitor model homes work the best.

"Geofencing is my #1, all-time, most-favorite tackle!"

Chapter 11
Best Tactics for
Offline and Print

*"The biggest challenge with offline
promotion is the reduced ability
to track results
and measure effectiveness."*

For obvious reasons, much of the marketing budget for new home builders is now devoted to digital channels where there is a greater ability to measure results and to trigger quick responses and action. However, there is still a place for offline and print marketing methods. And these traditional offline methods can be especially effective under certain circumstances. Offline impressions also tend to have a more emotional and lasting effect.

There are basically six advertising options or areas that fall under the category of offline and print. These include:

1. Newspaper Advertising
2. Magazine Advertising
3. Signage
4. Direct Mail
5. Radio (Chapter 12)
6. TV (Chapter 12)

Newspaper Advertising

Generally, we see that print ads work best when they are placed in newspapers with longer shelf lives and dedicated readership. Typically, this is a community newspaper that locals rely on for community updates, business services, and municipal news. There is also certain demographics that still support and read newspapers. This is typically the active adult, 55 and over demographic. Therefore, newspaper ads could be a good way to connect with local buyers, especially if your development is appealing to this age group.

The biggest challenge with offline promotion is the reduced ability to track results and to measure effectiveness. The key is to enable print to web activity and measure it. The best way to do this is with vanity URLs in order to track responses to each specific print campaign. These URLs can also be complemented by a trackable phone number used specifically for that lead source. Your onsite Sales team should also be alerted to the ad run to monitor for any surges in traffic triggered by the print ads.

Usually, a daily newspaper can produce a surge of activity within 24 to 48 hours of publication making a cause and effect of activity that can likely be attributed to the promotion.

The best uses for print ads are to announce:
- Grand Openings and Launches
- Special Sales & Promotions
- Open Houses
- Special Events

Magazine Advertising

The primary reason for advertising in magazines is brand awareness and to become relevant. If you are going to devote some of your marketing budget to magazine ads, you want to make sure you actually get noticed, or the expense isn't worth it. That means you should "go big" and choose a full-page color ad and buy the best placements. Best placements being the inside front, the inside back, and the back cover. This is necessary to get you the most exposure. However, you must also first determine that the target readership is in alignment with your target buyer profile. Magazine ads work very well for a new community launch or launch of a new phase.

Your ad must present a clear and differentiating message and speak directly to what the offer is. Your call to action should also be clear and in a way that will allow you to measure the engagement. Similar to newspaper ads, magazine advertising must also be done in a way that enables tracking and print to web activity. Just as with newspaper ads, you can use vanity URLs and a dedicated phone number to track responses. Your onsite team will also need to track any traffic attributable to the magazine promotion.

The New North

North McAllen has a new master-planned community that is making waves. With an island amphitheater, fiber-bundled technology and one of the largest community trail systems in the US, this community is unrivaled anywhere in the country.

Reserve your dream home today, before someone else does.

Homes from $180's to $1m+ · 956.205.0605 · TresLagosHomes.com

Your cost per lead with magazine ads might by 4X higher than the cost of a digitally sourced lead. However, the quality could be significantly higher as well. The reality is that when a prospect makes the effort to go to their mobile phone, tablet, or computer, manually type in a URL to get more information or manually dial a number to connect, this means they have high intent. There's no mouse to make action effortless and no chance of an impulse click. They are interested and motivated enough to transition from print to digital or to call. That's a great lead.

Direct Mail

There was a time when people received volumes of junk mail in their physical mail boxes. But once the internet and email became an option, many marketers opted for the much less expensive option of sending bulk advertising digitally. Volumes of email replaced volumes of snail mail. As a result, mail boxes are leaner these days. There's less printed junk to sift through and an improved chance for interesting mail to stand out. People, especially 55 and over active adults, are more likely to pay more attention and sift through their mail to look for the good stuff. For second or luxury home destination real estate offers, we find that business reply cards still can work effectively under the right circumstances and should be worth some consideration.

Again, this offline marketing option works best when promoting a specific event, an opening, a preview or first-look opportunity. There needs to be a specific reason or a specific time window to trigger action and yield the best results. We recommend an oversized 6x10 postcard to stand out. Cost-wise this could run 60-70¢ each for list, print, and postage.

The most important factor in direct mail is making sure you are using the right list. This could be hit or miss without targeting the ideal demographics for your development. You can filter lists by household income, age, zip codes, location, and more. Tracking must also be considered. With postcards, you can require that they bring the card for access or to redeem a special offer.

Another consideration is the value of familiarity. Just as with remarketing online, it is beneficial for people to receive multiple mailings to boost familiarity, interest, and action. In some cases, we suggest 4 mailings to the same group to build brand awareness and motivate action.

Another way you can improve results and lower costs is to do a saturation mailing. This saves you the cost of renting a list. The post office allows you to do a saturation mailing to all addresses in a defined area. It is like geofencing for mailing. You can choose specific office buildings, streets, zips, and neighborhoods with prospects that match your ideal demographics. The post office will then deliver your mailing to every mail box in the area with reduced postage rates.

Signage

Signage (billboards and outdoor media) are probably at the bottom of the list when we map out a marketing strategy. The costs are high, and the impact can be hard to measure. Nonetheless, if you decide to utilize some of your budget for signage, this is what I would recommend.

The best use of a billboard sign is to signal a directional exit to help motorists know where to exit or turn to get to your development. This means that adding marketing components like a URL or phone number are not helpful. You need to realize the speed of travel and the limited time people have to digest the information presented and the time to take action. In this function as a directional, a sign can be very helpful in drawing attention and triggering impulse traffic to your development. You can sometimes add overhangs at the top or bottom of the sign which helps to get attention. In these spots you might be able to add a URL or phone number to track some inquiries. But keep things easy to read and simple. There is a minimal amount of data that someone can intake while traveling in a moving car. The best option is a simple and easy to remember web address. Signs for a new community should be tied with a URL and landing page to capture sign-ups for an interest list and is a must have of any "fisherman." It is the staple of every real estate project.

Another possible sign placement is in front of the community development simply for a long-term branding and awareness play. This may be to announce the site of a future development too. But there needs to be a strategy to capture leads of potential buyers.

Billboards make sense for brand awareness for a new community if they are a directional with severe impact such as direct turn off a major highway or intersection. However, it should not be considered a top priority if there are budget constraints. National builders can afford it because typically corporate has a national fund and they have to use the money on something in-market marketers are not doing. Again, sometimes including unique URLs on signage can be difficult, but if you can at least include a unique number to gauge impact, do it.

Billboards can cost from $1,000 to $10,000 per month. In the end, the cost may not justify the purpose. To save, you may opt for billboards with rotating messages to promote multiple locations in your market.

All of these traditional print/offline options are not the highest on our priority list. They are difficult to measure and have less direct impact on trackable home sales. Nonetheless, they do have a place in contributing to a comprehensive marketing strategy.

The key tips here are assuring that you can enable print to web trackable URLs and phone numbers or write up an offer that requires bringing the flyer in for newspaper and magazine ads. Direct mail cannot be one and done. You should always do 2-3 mailings to the demographic, especially if you get significant response the first time around. Also, the U.S. post office offers a product called saturation mailing which is typically a great solution for farming adjacent communities and unique demographics that allows you to save as much as 30% on direct mail. And finally, art work and call to actions matter and can make a difference in response by as much as 50%.

"What's that Grandpa?"
"A newspaper."
"What's a newspaper?"
"..."

(Robert "Tito" Cowes Jr.)

Chapter 12
Best Tactics for
Radio and TV

"If you're going to invest in this channel,
it helps to involve digital counterparts
to push trackable traffic to your call to action."

Over the last 20 years, radio and TV have traditionally been among the top 5 ways to promote and advertise new homes and residential communities. With the onset and availability of several more effective technology driven promotional methods, this is no longer the case. There is still a place for radio and TV in real estate marketing, but they are now much further down on the playbook's priority list.

If you decide to tap into these traditional waters to fish for buyers, the primary challenge is measuring performance. There needs to be some aspect that enables you to quantify how many buyers were influenced by the ad. The most helpful enhancement to these marketing channels is that they have evolved to include digital counterparts, making measurement more feasible.

Radio Advertising – Best Practices

What we have found is that when a campaign is event driven, there are more opportunities to measure the impact. What works best are ads that promote an event, a grand opening, a special sale, a milestone celebration, or something like a pre-sale (get on the list) campaign. This enables the onsite Sales team to identify the source of surges in traffic triggered by the ad drop.

Another innovative development on this channel has been the emergence of alternate radio options. Beyond the regular AM and FM frequencies, there are now numerous online digital channels and programs that offer advertising opportunities. This provides sound-based and online clickable ads. Services such as Pandora and Spotify are leaders in building online radio/music networks that combine voice and click ads. This allows for better measurement options to quantify the impact of an ad campaign.

So, radio advertising can be effective but there must be some capability to track and push traffic to take action. Without the ability to track clicks via online affiliate sites, there must be some way to direct traffic to a trackable action. Vanity URLs and phone numbers can help. If no click feature is available, a voice ad should direct the listener to take some specific action so that the lead can be harvested and documented. As explained in the offline print ad chapter, when a person takes action that moves them from a non-digital connection to a digital online engagement, that is a strong indicator of interest and intent.

TV Advertising – Best Practices

In the past, television was the number one place where builders wanted to advertise and be seen. But just like radio advertising, TV ads are similarly difficult to measure and quantify impact. These days there are some new options to explore in the TV realm.

One is the existence of real estate TV shows. There are shows with decent follower counts, that could make this an affordable endeavor. Ad spends could be $4-$6K per month for weekly repeat ad spots. We are also seeing some builders buying air time directly and producing their own shows to showcase their inventory of homes and their communities. These programs are 100% dedicated to the builder's brand. This can also be effective and affordable depending on time slot. Cable programming provides numerous channel options for programming slots. These are most affordable in the after peak and Saturday morning time slots. Ad spends could be about $3-$4K per week. Straight run TV ad spots are more costly and can be prohibitive. It is not unusual to see costs of $2-$3K per ad spot in peak time slots.

The key with TV promotion is to invest in great video production. Visuals will directly affect the impact of the ad. And just like with radio, it is important for TV channels to work in tandem with their digital counterparts to boost lead development and measurement.

The Emergence of OTT

OTT refers to over-the-top audio and visual programming that is delivered over the internet instead of through an MSO (multiple-system operator). Prime examples of OTT service providers include Hulu, Amazon Video, and Sling TV. Generally, the free versions of these streaming services, include ads that cannot be bypassed, delivering a captive audience. This allows advertisers to promote via a more intentful and less wasteful version of TV. The availability of demographics profiles, behavioral data, and measurable stats makes OTT better than TV.

The key takeaways regarding radio and TV channels are that there must be a deliberate attempt to measure impact. If you are going to invest in this channel, it helps to involve digital counterparts to push trackable traffic to your call to action. Your Sales team can also track surges in traffic that are linked to ad runs, while vanity URLs and phone numbers can provide additional data for your analytics. If you can afford it, they still remain the most powerful and lasting brand builder. Unfortunately, it is still amongst the hardest to measure engagement.

"OTT is the new way to bait streamers."

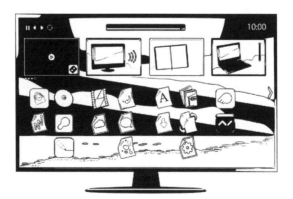

Chapter 13
Realtor Marketing Strategies

"At the end of the day,
we all need to be aligned
with realtors in the mix."

Realtors are an integral part of real estate marketing for new home developments and single-family homes. Historically, the range of transactions with realtor representation tend to be around 30% on the low end and 95% on the high end. The builders at 95% rely almost completely on realtor referrals. Other builders who focus on having their own Sales team and in-house sales efforts, only rely on realtors on average about 40% of their transactions. The key questions for a builder are: What is your reliance on realtors? And are their opportunities to expand your own Sales force and your own predictable lead generation program?

If you decide to invest in your own fishing/lead generation program, your reliance on realtors should no longer be in the 90% and above range. A healthy expectation with a lead-driven team working on your own cultivated buyer leads, might reduce your realtor represented transactions to about 60%. There should really be an effort to sell at least 50% of your inventory directly yourself, especially since most buyers are doing the work to research and find what they want themselves. They will only bring a realtor into the mix if they need advice. Buyers can also receive incentives (builder concessions) to proceed without a realtor—thus reducing realtor commissions. However, at the end of the day, we all need to be aligned with realtors in the mix. Even if you are on the lower 30% side, 30% is still a huge chunk of transactions. Realtors are a natural extension of the Sales' arm.

The challenge for builders is to establish a perfect balance that integrates multiple sales channels along with quality realtor relationships.

There are two kinds of buyers: Buyers that want realtors to do all of the work for them and buyers who prefer to do their own homework to narrow down what they are looking for. This second type of buyer reduces realtor commissions in the transaction and could earn builder concessions for the buyer. A lead driven sales organization should rely around 50% or less on realtors generating buyers.

There are certain markets where realtor relationships are indispensable. In those, you want to have more realtor specific marketing programs such as drips or loyalty reward programs.

Nurturing Realtor Relationships

Some of the primary ways to build connections with realtors are to make sure they are aware of your inventory and to start to nurture these important relationships by:

- **Email Marketing** – Association lists can help to build propriety opt-in lists of realtors that are interested in your developments and bring you buyers. Email marketing is cost effective and direct. Drip email campaigns can also help to keep realtors engaged and aware of your value proposition.

- **Advertisements in Realtor Industry Magazines** – These magazines provide offline and online methods to connect and provide editorial content for realtors that showcase new home builders.

- **Realtor Driven Websites** – For example, New Home Source Professional and Builders Update can provide access to realtors looking to have exclusive access to new home inventory before it hits the MLS and general access. Realtor driven websites are good for pre-sells as well.

- **Networking** – The most effective method could prove to be the efforts of your own onsite Sales team to network and connect directly with realtors and realty offices in your markets. This assures that they are aware of your available inventory and have more personal connection.

- **Builder Rewards Programs** – The programs create realtor loyalty and encourage more transactions.

Realtor showcases, educational events, and grassroot realtor office presentations are very effective as are check-ins. The latest trend is using content marketing with instructions on how to conduct transactions in your organization. Driving awareness to this content—specifically to channels realtors are on, such as local MLSs and social media—can really drive the point home.

As marketers, we should not assume all markets are the same. In comparison to Texas, where most home builders provide estimates and pricing on a new home up front as well as onsite or nearby selection centers like in Mississippi, when a person buys a new home, typically they will not have a final sales price until after they go to multiple vendor storefront sites and make their final decorating selections. Providing realtors with this information upfront, makes interacting with your company easier and makes them experts to their clients.

The key is to nurture and manage a good list of realtors that can bring you buyers. Mass mailing huge lists of realtors can be costly and ineffective. Your best list is the one that you grow internally from opt-in emails, newspaper ads, online, social media, a local realtor publication, or through your own grassroots program. These will be realtors that bring you referrals and buyers. The challenge is to keep them informed and aware of your value proposition. Realtors need to be an integral part of your strategy. The goal is to nurture realtors that can bring you buyers instead of you giving them rewards simply for representing your buyers.

"I'll provide you with the bait, but you have to give me 50% of your fish in return."

Chapter 14
CRM –
Marketing Automation

"Marketing Automation provides
powerful functions and reporting
but only if it is used."

Marketing automation is an important factor in enhancing communications between the builder and the buyer. It provides a mechanism to automate and expose engagements from your leads and buyers. Because of this, marketing automation has emerged as a critical tool in optimizing your Customer Relationship Management (CRM) and sales machine.

CRM and marketing automation solutions can automate action-based workflows by aggregating the capture of leads from different sources such as your own website, Facebook and other social media, listing sites such as Zillow or New Home Source, as well as automating communication follow up and assignment of activities for sales. The key to effectiveness is the implementation and alignment of the lead follow-up process with automated workflows and tracking of data. Training Sales on how to properly use the CRM is also key.

At a minimum, your CRM needs to:

- Capture your leads
- Distribute them to the appropriate sales people in a timely manner
- Track the source of the lead - for example:
  - Model/Onsite/Walk-in (but attempt to further identify the original lead source)
  - Online (Website, Google, Social Media, Banner Ad, Etc.)
  - Aggregated Lead Adaptors (such as a listing website)
  - Print, Radio, TV
- Manage the communication after capture – for example:
  - Record Notes
  - Set Appointments
  - Facilitate Calendar Integration
  - Initiate a Drip Campaign
  - Enable Reports (Traffic, Sales, Pipeline, Etc.)

Marketing automation provides powerful functions and reporting but only if it is used. We estimate that 50% of builder Sales teams barely utilize their CRM and reluctantly use it only because they are required to. They are not taking full advantage of the ability to farm and nurture the database for home sales. Generally, only 25% of Sales team members are power users. They "get it" and use their CRM to drive results. The most successful builder Sales teams have 100% participation and all team members are required to use the CRM. It is part of their everyday job to keep the CRM up to date and capable of providing important intelligence, including the ability to predict sales versus only marketing activities.

A little over a decade ago, while working with and serving new home builders and developers, my business partner and I were looking for a soup-to-nuts solution that could integrate with other solution providers. We realized that there were no real solutions in the marketplace where you could do lead management (CRM), marketing campaign management, contract management, and production orders, all in one system.

That's why we developed SmartTouch® NexGen, customized to meet the needs of new home builders and developers. We are the first to implement a marketing automation mechanism driven by custom workflows based on engagement driven actions. It is very powerful in delivering personalized content, lead scoring, and triggering automated functions to nurture each lead through the sales funnel to the closing table.

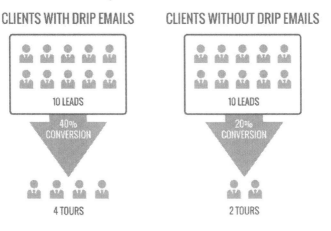

The goal with marketing automation is to make sure no lead gets left behind. We can now help our clients to optimize their integrated efforts, and that means more buyers are found and more homes are sold. If you are going to spend any money on any marketing channel (fishing in all of these different waters to find buyers) we have discussed, a CRM is a must. SmartTouch® NexGen is like a secret weapon in your tackle box that can ultimately be the centerpiece to a powerful and effective sales and marketing operation.

The future of these solutions lies in automating the execution of the most effective sales and marketing workflows. CRMs are the front end of the process. Integration with sales purchase contracts and ERPs, facilitated mobile apps that are more user-friendly for Sales people, and appending data with more profile data are amongst the innovations and effective technology initiatives emerging in this market segment.

"Having all my catches in one CRM significantly reduces my risk of accidently letting one loose."

Chapter 15
Sales and Marketing
Integration

"Sales and Marketing
are not designed to operate independently.
Neither can truly be successful
without the other."

Probably one of the most overlooked and most important communications that take place in any business is the connection between the Sales Team and the Marketing Team. Sales and Marketing must be integrated to optimize potential sales results for your entire development. The key to a successful sales system is to be sure that both Sales and Marketing are in alignment and connected. And that can only happen if there are established channels of communication so that these two critical components to your success are working in tandem for maximum results.

The Marketing Team

There must be transparency in the marketing department. Your Sales Team needs to know what advertising channels are being used and what the messaging is in the marketplace. If the Sales Team doesn't know when to expect bursts of traffic or inquiries, how can they be prepared to maximize results with those fresh leads? And they can only be effective in reporting the field results from all marketing and advertising if they are aware of what campaigns are running.

Equally as important, is developing a content marketing strategy that differentiates from the traditional seasonal and sales promotion. Marketing must produce content around your unique value proposition and buyer demographics.

The Sales Team

The Sales Team must also do their part by working the leads and traffic generated by the Marketing Team's efforts. They should be screening and tracking the source of all lead activity and report that data back to the Marketing Team, so Marketing can optimize what's working and what's not to drive more leads back to the onsite Sales Team.

It is the responsibility of the field team to determine and map out how any potential buyers started and continued their engagement with the development. Was it due to an organic online search, a landing page, chat session, phone call, a text message, a billboard sign, etc.?

The more you learn about the journey a buyer took to get to your model home, the more likely you are to improve marketing efforts and ROI. Feedback from Sales on the quality of leads by sources is also critical. Sometimes a top lead generating source is not the top source of actual onsite visits, showings, or tours, which should also influence marketing decisions.

It will take initiative and effort to bring these two key groups into alignment. Sometimes the biggest challenge is that these two forces are physically separated from each other. Usually the Marketing Team is in some corporate office location that might not even be in the same city, and the Sales Team is onsite at the development.

This is why there must be a deliberate effort to create and maintain a communication channel between these two primary drivers of sales.

It is important that whenever Marketing launches an advertising campaign, that sales is in the loop. They need to be aware of when a campaign is launching, who it is directed at, and they need to know the messaging of the promotion. The whole process becomes even more successful when Sales participates in the development of the campaign. This gives them some buy-in as well as an opportunity to contribute their insights from the field. This way when a marketing campaign launches, everyone is aligned and ready to take action. When the right hand knows what the left hand is doing and vice versa, there are no surprises and they can work hand in hand to generate the best return on investment.

We have seen marketing campaigns of all types that weren't communicated with the Sales Team. Then the Sales crew is blindsided by buyers and realtors instead of being prepared for the opportunity. If you expect Sales to maximize marketing effectiveness while working on the frontlines, but you blindfold them by not informing them about what is coming, you can't expect to get the best results possible.

The simple solution is communication. For one, Sales should be engaged in the brainstorming and ideation process. Before launch, whether digital or offline, Sales should have a copy of the promotion, so they know what is being launched. They should know what is happening, who is targeted, when will it be launched and what is the message.

To make this relationship truly work, Sales must also do their part. They must embrace the CRM and document the results of all Marketing efforts. They need to help Marketing know what strategies work best and who are the best target markets. They must carefully identify and document the true source or journey of every lead. When aligned, both forces are better prepared to leverage the other's insights and further optimize and improve the brand message.

Sales and Marketing are not designed to operate independently.

Neither can truly be successful without the other. When these two departments understand and value the role each plays in the sales process and are accountable to each other, that's when you'll have a fully functioning sales machine and your new home sales results will be significantly higher.

You can have the best bait in town (Marketing and Advertising) but if you don't have the fishing hooks (Sales Team) to catch the fish coming to eat your bait, then you won't catch anything. Likewise, you can have the best fishing hooks that money can buy, but if you stick those hooks in the water without any bait, don't expect to be eating fish for dinner.

"Which is more important: the bait or the hook?"

Chapter 16
Predicting, Measuring, Optimizing, and Accountability

"By enabling the measure
of every cost and action,
you can ultimately start to understand
and study your conversion rates."

The biggest step in taking your business to the next level involves strategizing to become a lead generation and numbers-driven type of organization. The concept of developing a strategic and predictive performance modeling plan is about being able to put together a program in which you can begin to predict and forecast sales.

Predictive Performance Modeling Is...

A financial model, based on conversion metrics, designed to help us calculate what you need to spend - and where – to achieve your sales goals.

It all begins with your marketing investments. This is set initially by allocating anywhere from .5 to 2% of gross revenue. The amount will differ based on competition, volume, demand, if it is the first year of the development's launch or year five of building, etc.

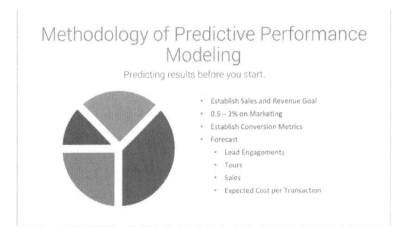

All of your variables will determine the appropriate amount to spend. Your marketing plan will encompass operating obligations as well as all of the marketing channels utilized.

This could include:

- CRM fees
- Creative fees to agencies
- Management of digital advertising such as social media, geofencing, media buys, and search engine marketing
- Website creation, maintenance, optimization, and updates
- Printing of collateral and signs
- Microsites and landing pages
- Digital ad banners (which should be updated at least once a quarter).
- SEO and Google business listings
- And all other channels utilized and outlined in this book

Cost per Engagement (now also being called action)

When we look at cost per engagement for a new primary home residence, we must look at all of the tactics within the marketing plan that facilitated the engagement. Engagement activities include:

- An online registration
- A walk-in/onsite visit
- Registered traffic
- Discussion with a salesperson
- A phone call to a call center or directly to the community
- Online chat inquiry
- Text message

Each tactic within the plan plays a role in attracting an engagement with a builder or community. This includes:

- SEO & SEM
- Geofencing
- Publisher listing websites
- Offline/online magazines and newspapers
- Outdoor media, billboards, and signage
- Broadcast media – Radio & TV
- Digital tools – video & social media
- Direct mail

The primary task is to start studying and measuring. And by enabling the measure of every cost and action, you can ultimately start to understand and study your conversion rates.

A typical plan that we might put together for a client for a new home residence community might have the following results: For every 10 lead engagements, on average 2 will lead to an onsite visit. A visit to either the model or sales office are counted as a visit. From there we look at models. There are differences depending on the home. Generally, the conversion rates are higher for homes under $500,000.

Capture Rates

The next concern is to establish how many onsite visits can be converted to a home sale. So, on average we estimate that every 100 visits to a model home converts to 15 sales. That makes our capture rate 15% or 1.5 of every 10 onsite visits you get.

Building a Predictive Performance Modeling Formula

Once we know how many engagements convert to tours, and we know how many tours convert to home sales, we have enough data to drive a powerful sales machine. We can build a model that allows us to understand and utilize conversion rates.

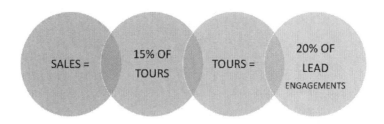

We can further explore the tactics that drive results within the predictive model. Using the data collected in the CRM, we can further define conversion rates by community, by sales agent, and by source. This is achieved by utilizing the tools at our disposal such as lead tracking, Google Analytics, and the Sales Team CRM updates and notes to gather correct data. The key is to not just track the medium (Facebook, online search, direct mail, etc.) that attracted the lead, but the call-to-action source (click-to-call, driving directions, form completed, etc.) as well.

Track actions with Google Analytics.

Track Lead Source through a home builder CRM.

The ultimate objective in tracking medium and source, is to enable the organization to fully understand conversion and capture rates, what activities are driving sales, and the ability to predict future sales with accuracy based on these conversion attributes quarter over quarter. This also helps the organization to identify areas of waste and make better investments in marketing tactics, thus reducing the cost to market. Everything is optimized to produce the most efficient cost per lead, cost per tour, and cost per sale. This accelerates the entire sales operation so that *no lead is left behind.*

Over the long term, this data analysis allows us to measure and predict performance. We can start to produce rolling forecasts from quarter to quarter based on historical data. We can also learn more about buyer preferences and how long it takes for a lead to get from first engagement to closing. This is powerful information that can drive current efforts and predict future results. That is, we can predict how a boost in leads today might translate into X amount of closings Y months from now. This becomes a tracking system with the potential to assess, evaluate, and predict future performance in the pipeline.

The endgame is having a measured approach. This is possible when we have tactical execution in place for all parts of the plan. Having "all lines in" is understanding the big picture and being able to truly optimize your sales operation to predict sales and ultimately, grow your business to where you want it to be.

"We won't know who caught the bigger fish unless we measure them."

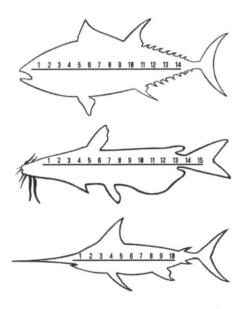

Chapter 17
The Future of Fishing for Buyers

"The builders and developers
that offer this level of personalization
and interactive experience
will have a clear advantage."

Many of the tools we see today to drive sales efforts will continue to dominate the marketing arena. However, you can expect the capabilities of these tools to expand, and consumer expectations will expand with them.

Listing websites will continue to improve in sophistication. Builder and developer websites must be able to offer customization of plans, finishes, and all features going into personalization as well. Think about what is possible on an automaker's website. You can select and order your vehicle down to the last detail.

Consumers will eventually expect that same level of customize and order ease when purchasing a new home. They will demand to have the same level of control and buyer experience. That is where the market is going—an experience just like buying a retail product on Amazon—where you have countless pictures, reviews, videos, details, and online interaction.

The true future is offering buyers the opportunity to buy a home virtually, including paperwork, deposit, and closing documents. At some point, (and already occurring in some markets such as the Greater Toronto Area and to become an expected option in the next decade) consumers will be able to complete an entire home purchase online. The entire experience that would have happen in-person and onsite, will happen with an online model home. The buyer will customize and view the rendering of their selections all online. The builders and developers that offer this level of personalization and interactive experience will have a clear advantage.

This consumer experience trend fully substantiates investment in tools to facilitate the interactive and personalized experience that consumers want. This includes widgets, interactive floor plans, and other online tools to expedite the buying process and transaction.

(https://www.blackburncommunities.com/new-homes/tx/austin/ the-crossing-at-wells-branch/hamilton/24345/)

Builders Digital Experience (BDX) also just launched a new web property that allows users to find a home by selecting images of rooms they like and through the algorithm it customizes the search results to homes that match the criteria.

Internet search and search engines will continue to be a powerful tool to enable consumers to begin their home buying research and transaction. Expect consumers to have access to a growing list of devices that can be used to connect to online resources. This will impact the types of marketing campaigns that builders and developers must create to be adaptable to multiple platforms.

Think mobile first. All content must be mobile-friendly.

Listing websites are expected to continue being a key tool for buyers to use to seek and compare their options. Expect these sites to transform to a more adaptive "Amazon-like" experience with enhanced compare-contrast-recommend features. This includes a higher level of personalization and an expedited transaction experience.

One likely development that makes many feel a bit uneasy, is the role that artificial intelligence (AI) will play in all future consumer transactions, including home sales. Image having a fully-programmed robot at your model home to help prospective buyers to initiate and complete the entire transaction. Your robot will know EVERY detail about your inventory, including options, pricing, scheduling, and more. Then your robot can get the transaction started, knowing every detail about all of the financial aspects of the transaction. The power of automation with robots already exists. So, expect to see it applied to home sales at some point in the near future.

However, the future that's happening right now is geofencing. Geofencing (see Chapter 10) is becoming one of the most powerful influencers in the marketing mix. We can now put ads in front of the exact people we are targeting. And we can drive traffic and action right now, not in a few hours, a few days, or even a few weeks – right now! We can use geofencing to get a prospect who is at your competitor's development, to leave and come to your site. That's powerful!

Of course, since this is so new, this marketing tool may evolve over the next few years, depending on privacy laws, legislative challenges, and other wrinkles in its path. We continue to monitor factors that could restrict geofencing. But for now, it truly is the future of digital marketing.

"I'm so good the fish line up to be caught!"

Chapter 18
Building and Launching
YOUR Playbook

"Having a reliable formula
is the HOLY GRAIL in
predictive performance modeling."

When you're ready to build and launch your marketing strategy playbook, the important thing to remember is that you don't have to "bite off the whole thing" at once, but it certainly helps to have all lines in!

The first step is clarifying all of the components that will go into your marketing strategy. Some organizations will count some basic foundational items as part of their marketing strategy, such as decorating expenses, signage, and sometimes promotional items that are shared with corporate and employees. Even model home expenses and marketing managers as a headcount can be considered an expense of your marketing strategy. Those things should be considered operating expenses and separated out when calculating your cost per divided by lead gen/advertising expenses.

But if you really want to measure the efficiency of your plan, you'll need to establish a percentage of gross sales to invest in multiple marketing channels, (as outlined throughout this book), and then measure the results of every invested dollar. You want to measure what your investment creates for you in <u>traffic</u>!

We recommend reviewing once a quarter and doing a deep-dive analysis of each tactic and looking at adjustments and optimizations to the marketing plan.

Then once you have this discipline in place you want to start looking at quarter over quarter, month to month, and annual trends within your overall KPIs (cost per lead engagement, cost per tour, cost per sale), Sales KPIs (lead to tour, tour to sales, contracts to closing), and Marketing KPIs (registrations, calls, driving direction).

So, your playbook will encompass digital media, offline media, direct mail, and possibly radio & TV. You'll then track and measure all traffic. Tracking is possible with services like Google Analytics and other tools built into the various channels. By tracking and measuring, you can determine the level of engagement from each of your investment channels. This enables you to understand, predict, and achieve conversions.

Just as important is having a Sales team that is committed to utilizing your CRM and recording all activities, onsite visits, engagements, and sales. This, combined with tracking and marketing integration, will help you to optimize your marketing plan. You'll be able to know what is needed to get a lead to become a tour and then to become a sale. This measurement and tracking ultimately allows you to understand and predict your business. Initially, we can predict on a macro level and then break it down to micro levels by community.

The next key to the success of the playbook is the ability to determine the average time duration from lead to sale. This is the lifecycle of the prospect. We can then predict that with X amount of leads today, we can expect Y sales, and Z period of time before closings.

Volume x Conversion Rate x Average Time to Close a Sale

This is a formula that helps us to hit all of our goals and predict the business! Having a reliable formula is the HOLY GRAIL in predictive performance modeling. Then with discipline, we look at the data, make revisions as appropriate. What develops is a powerful ability to see and predict trends from quarter to quarter.

Of course, you can make adjustments, based on facts and special situation spending (branding, market awareness, new project jumpstart). But what you will have is a playbook that drives down the cost per sale. You use FACTS and DATA to drive RESULTS. Ergo, yielding you optimal return on having *All Lines In!*

"I've caught my goal today.
Time to head back and start cooking."

Illustration & Image Credits

P.1 - Cover Illustration Image by Shawn Ng

P. 8 - Photo from Getty Images

P. 10 - Illustration from Getty Images

P. 13 - Illustration by SmartTouch® Interactive

P. 14 - Photo from Getty Images

*P. 16 - Illustration from Getty Images edited by SmartTouch®
Interactive*

P. 17 - Photo from Getty Images

*P. 20 - Illustration from Getty Images edited by SmartTouch®
Interactive*

*P. 22 - Photos from Getty Images; Video Example by Tres Lagos in
McAllen, Texas*

*P. 24-25 - Blog Post by Gardens at Verde Vista in Georgetown, Texas;
Facebook Page by Veramendi in New Braunfels, Texas; Google
Business Listing of Gardens at Verde Vista in Georgetown, Texas;
YouTube Channel by Tres Lagos in McAllen, Texas; Online
Interactive Plat Map from blackburncommunities.com; Floor Plan
Kiosk from Blackburn Communities' Gardens at Mayfield in
Georgetown, Texas community with SmartTouch® Team and Evie
Tavarez (Director of Business Development & Marketing)*

*P. 26 - Illustration from Getty Images edited by SmartTouch®
Interactive*

*P. 27 - Website Home Page of Blackburn Communities in Oxford,
Mississippi*

*P. 31 - Illustration from Getty Images edited by SmartTouch®
Interactive*

P. 33 - Example taken from Keywords Everywhere

P. 34 - Example taken from WordPress; Tres Lagos in McAllen, TX, website

P. 35 - Website Home Page of Tres Lagos in McAllen, Texas

P. 35 - Example taken from RGV New Homes Guide Online Magazine

P. 36 - XML Sitemap Example taken from Tres Lagos in McAllen, Texas website

P. 37 - Example taken from Google Search Page

P. 40 - Illustration by SmartTouch® Interactive

P. 41 - Example of Google Ads Negative Keyword Record

P. 43 - Illustration from Getty Images edited by SmartTouch® Interactive

P. 45 - Bentsen Palm in McAllen, Texas; Reengagement Email Campaign Example

P. 47 - Bentsen Palm in McAllen, Texas; Drip Email Example

P. 48 - Tres Lagos in McAllen, Texas, Drip Campaign Examples

P. 54 - Tres Lagos in McAllen, Texas, Email Campaign dissected by SmartTouch® Interactive

P. 55 - Sitterle Homes in San Antonio, Texas, Email Campaign dissected by SmartTouch® Interactive

P. 56 - Illustration from Getty Images edited by SmartTouch® Interactive

P. 57 - Facebook Post by SmartTouch® Interactive

P. 59 - Facebook Audience Targeting Infographic by SmartTouch® Interactive

P. 61 - Twitter Hashtag Example of Veramendi in New Braunfels, Texas; Instagram Desktop Grid Example of Veramendi in New Braunfels, Texas; Instagram Mobile Grid Example of Veramendi in New Braunfels, Texas

P. 62 - Pinterest Boards Example of The Lakes at Centerra in Loveland, Colorado

P. 63 - Facebook Event Page Example hosted Tres Lagos in McAllen, Texas

P. 64 - Illustration from Getty Images edited by SmartTouch® Interactive

P. 65 - Example taken from Google Search Results Page

P. 67 - Photos from Getty Images edited by SmartTouch® Interactive

P. 67 - Example from NewHomeSource.com of Sitterle Homes listing in Serene Hills

P. 68 - Illustration from Getty Images edited by SmartTouch® Interactive

P. 69 - Example from ESPN.com with Veramendi in New Braunfels, Texas, digital banner ad

P. 71 - Illustration from Getty Images edited by SmartTouch® Interactive

P. 73 - SmartTouch® Geo logo designed by SmartTouch® Interactive

P. 74 - SmartTouch® Geo banner ad examples of Gardens at Verde Vista in Georgetown, Texas.

P. 75 - Photo of Toyota Highlander in Cedar Park, Texas, taken by Robert Cowes III.

P. 76-77 - Infographics by SmartTouch® Interactive and Conversion Zone example from SmartTouch® Geo Report

P. 78 - Photo from Getty Images with Gardens at Verde Vista in Georgetown, Texas, geofencing banner ad. Image edited by SmartTouch® Interactive

P. 79 - Illustration from Getty Images edited by SmartTouch® Interactive

P. 81 - Print Ad Example of Gardens at Verde Vista in Georgetown, Texas

P. 83 - Print Ad Example of Tres Lagos in McAllen, Texas

P. 85 - Directional Billboard Example of Tres Lagos in McAllen, Texas

P. 86 - Community Signage Examples of The Preserve at Mayfield Ranch in Round Rock, Texas

P. 87 - Robert "Tito" Cowes Jr. reading a newspaper

P. 88 - Illustration from Getty Images edited by SmartTouch® Interactive

P. 89 - HotOn! Homes logo; hotonhomes.com

P. 90 - Photo from Getty Images

P. 91 - Illustration from Getty Images edited by SmartTouch® Interactive

P. 95 - Saratoga Homes in Houston, Texas, Realtor Email Example; The Lakes at Centerra in Loveland, Colorado, Realtor Reengagement Email Example

P. 96 - Illustration from Getty Images edited by SmartTouch® Interactive

P. 97 - SmartTouch® NexGen desktop graphic by SmartTouch® Interactive

P. 98 - Infographic by SmartTouch® Interactive

P. 99 - Infographic by SmartTouch® Interactive

P. 100 - Saratoga Homes in Houston, Texas area; Persona Email Examples

P. 101 - Illustration from Getty Images edited by SmartTouch® Interactive

P. 102 - Illustration from Getty Images edited by SmartTouch® Interactive

P. 103 - Photo from Getty Images edited by SmartTouch® Interactive

P. 104 - Infographic by SmartTouch® Interactive

P. 106 - Illustration from Getty Images edited by SmartTouch® Interactive

P. 107 - Predictive Performance Modeling definition by SmartTouch® Interactive

P. 108 - Methodology of Predictive Performance Modeling developed by SmartTouch® Interactive

P. 110 - Illustration by SmartTouch® Interactive

P. 111 - Home Builder CRM infographic by SmartTouch® Interactive; Event Label Examples taken from Google Analytics

P. 112 - Illustration from Getty Images edited by SmartTouch® Interactive

P. 114 - Interactive Floor Plan Example from Blackburn Communities Website

P. 115 - Photos from Getty Image with Gardens at Verde Vista in Georgetown, Texas geofencing banner ad; Image edited by SmartTouch® Interactive

P. 116 - Illustration from Getty Images edited by SmartTouch® Interactive

P. 119 - Illustration from Getty Images edited by SmartTouch® Interactive

About the Author
Robert Cowes III

Originally from Panama, Robert Cowes III is a former college and semi-pro baseball player turned real estate lead gen marketer with a BBA in Finance & Marketing from St. Edward's University and an MBA from Texas State International Business.

As President and CEO of SmartTouch® Interactive, an award-winning software and digital marketing agency founded in 2010, Robert specializes in the unique needs of the real estate industry. In less than a decade, SmartTouch®'s lead generation programs have generated over 1 million leads and nurtured over 250,000 prospects that have led to over 2 billion in sales.

Robert is an entrepreneur and 20-year marketing veteran with expertise in product management, design and execution of lead generation programs, branding, and account service. With a deep expertise and specialty in digital marketing and results-driven lead gen campaigns, Robert develops marketing programs for residential home builders and developers that consistently get results, generate leads, and elicit sales.

Outside of developing successful marketing programs, Robert has stayed involved in professional associations throughout his career, serving on the Board of Directors for the Austin Home Builders Association for 3 years as well as serving on the Sales & Marketing Council for the National Home Builders Association and also as VP of Collegiate Relations for the American Marketing Association Austin Chapter.

Robert lives in Austin, Texas with his wife, Norma Guerrero Cowes and son Roberto Carlos.

About
SmartTouch® Interactive

SmartTouch® Interactive is an innovative digital marketing agency dedicated to helping residential home builders and developers connect with their ideal buyer by generating quality leads and nurturing those leads to sale—all with a focus on accountable ROI.

SmartTouch®'s innovation in lead generation and digital marketing supports home builders and residential developers meet their goals year over year. Setting a new standard, the company is a single-solution digital marketing provider solving the need for proven lead generation programs; a lead nurturing CRM/Marketing Automation platform, SmartTouch® NexGen; and a cutting-edge homebuyer geofencing solution, SmartTouch® Geo.

SmartTouch® is a data driven company and excels at putting data to leads, tours, and sales; reporting on campaigns every step of the way to make sure home builders and developers are getting the most out of their marketing dollars.

How to Contact Robert

Was this playbook helpful to your organization?
Need a guide to go All Lines In and sell more homes faster?

Contact Robert Cowes III,
CEO & President of SmartTouch® Interactive

Phone: (512) 659-6863
Email: rcowes@smarttouchinteractive.com
Website: www.smarttouchinteractive.com

SmartTouch® Interactive
8500 Shoal Creek Blvd
Bldg. 4, Ste 100
Austin, TX 78757

To purchase bulk copies of this book at a discount for your Sales and Marketing teams, please contact SmartTouch® Interactive:

smart@smarttouchinteractive.com or (512) 582-5900

Made in the USA
Columbia, SC
29 February 2020